THE REALITY CREATION TECHNIQUE

FREDERICK E. DODSON

COPYRIGHT

The Copyright of this work lies with the author. Any unauthorized reproduction without the authors written consent, will be handled legally.

DISCLAIMER

The author is not responsible for effects readers have or allegedly have from this book, just like a driving school instructor is not responsible for his students driving. Furthermore, the information provided in this book is not a substitute for conventional medical assistance.

.

CONTENTS

CHAPTER ONE

REALITY CREATION BY PERSONAL WILL

Intention & Counter-Intention

The Technique is a psycho-spiritual tool that will support you in creating the reality you prefer in life. This technique is the answer to the frequently-asked-question *"If I practice only one thing for the rest of my life, what technique should it be?"*

As a life coach I often recommend to my students to take just **one** practice, one method, one technique, one style and practice that until it begins creating results and change. What matters more than the specific method is the full commitment of the student to learn one thing properly instead of nervously jumping from one tool to another, one book to another, one philosophy to another. The Reality Creation Technique was created for those who are looking for that one tool that covers it all – the practical and the mystical, the peace and prosperity.

The Reality Creation Technique is extremely simple and consists of two steps:

- State Your Intention

- Release Counter-Intentions

Alternate between 1 and 2 until there are no counter-intentions, meaning the reality you intended to manifest has manifested.

That's all folks, thanks for reading! ☺

State Your Intention

Except that 99.9% of humanity can't handle that simplicity not to mention believe in it. Which I why the rest of this booklet will be spent explaining the technique, detailing it, giving examples and variations.

Here are some examples for Intentions one could state:

"I have the best vacation of my life"

"I allow myself to make $15 000 Dollars a month with ease"

"I have a healthy and athletic body"

"I am a vibrant and successful lawyer"

"I win the race on Friday"

"I find the job that is just-right-for-me"

"I allow myself to find just the right partner for me this weekend"

3

The wording "I want" is indicative of lack and not permissible. "I will" is no good either because it projects the preferred reality into the Future. "I have" is good, "I am" even better. "I decide" captures the spirit of an intention and is also highly recommended. "I allow" is very popular among practitioners of the technique because reality creation is more of an allowing than a forcing. Stick to one of these phrasings for your Intentions and you'll be just fine.

An Intention brings up its Opposite

The intentions you choose should go from realistic and close-to-you in the beginning, to more advanced and high-up over the years, as you grow stronger and more-confident. If you have never manifested $15 000 by the power of your word alone, or if you haven't even manifested it by conventional means, then that would probably be too high as a starting point. Start with manifesting $100 by intention alone. Once you've actually manifested $100, move up to $500 and then to

$1000. Then, perhaps, do another $1000, just to acquaint your body-mind with the new, awesome ability. The mind is easily overwhelmed, so don't push it. Yes, challenge yourself plenty, but don't overdo it. If you've manifested $1000 twice it's probably safe to move up to $5000 and then $10 000. In no case should you move up higher without having achieved the prior.

If you don't want any problems in life, don't have any goals or intentions. Every time you do form an Intention, it automatically brings up whatever stands in the way of that. I'm quite serious when saying that you will be happy and free of all difficulty if you have no goals at all. But having goals and achieving them is a lot of fun and allows for an entirely different type of happiness not experienced by that many.

As a rule of the thumb, know that the higher up your goal and the more specific your goal, the more blocks, problems, objections, resistance and doubts it will bring up. Money being on most peoples minds let me use its example again:

"I allow myself to have $100 Dollars with ease" does not bring up much resistance because anyone can easily imagine having $100. Also, it is not specified when that money will manifest. This is way too easy, even for you and I don't recommend that as a starting-point. Instead, spike up the challenge a bit by intending:

"I allow myself to have $100 Dollars with ease this week". Being this specific brings up more doubts and resistances but since the goal is still not way up there, it's still something you can handle.

If "I allow myself to have $1000 Dollars with ease this week" is too much to handle for the mind, then try "I allow myself to have $1000 Dollars with ease this month".

"I allow myself to have $1000 Dollars in a rolled-up-cash-bundle within the next 5 minutes" is so specific that it is probably not appropriate for anyone but the most wizardly sage. More often being too specific is an indicator that someone is ego-run rather than allowing "the Universe" (life, the energy-field, God) to manifest the Intention. Often only someone attempting to prove "how great" he is would have that kind of intention. Trying to prove your skills to others is a no-no. It's best to keep much of your Intention-Creating to yourself. Becoming extremely specific as to try to work "magic" is a no-no. As we will later explain it is something much greater than you, that's actually doing the creating.

Make sure you have your Intention right the first time because *The Reality Creation Technique* does not permit a change of the Intention once it is launched. The desire to change the Intention is handled as another of many forms of doubt and resistance.

Its not a Desire, it's a Decision

Once you are sure about your Intention, voice it. Voice it as a *Decision*. A Decision feels very different than a Desire, a Wish, a Dream or even a Goal. A Decision says "this is the way it is!" and then that's the way it is. A Decision means that you your 100% willing to choose reality A and abandon reality B, never looking back to B. A Decision implies that there are no ifs and buts, although the second step of "Releasing Counter-Intentions" will handle such ifs and buts anyway. Oftentimes the mere Decision, the mere *Willingness* (as opposed to Wanting-ness, which is actually Lackful-ness) is enough to either have the Intention manifest or put you on a path to the goal. But for cases in which manifestation is not apparent the second step comes into play.

Types of Counter-Intentions

The second step after voicing your Intention is to "release counter-intentions". Counter-Intention is my word-creation to describe objections, doubts, problems, resistances, blocks, issues, second-thoughts, matters arising, beliefs, emotions, sensations, feelings and realities that are in contradiction to your Intention. The Reality Creation Technique asks you to never handle problems outside of the context of an Intention again. Behind every problem you have there is an Intention. Do not see the two things separately. So if having no money is the problem, somewhere there must be an intention to have money, otherwise having no money would be no problem. Intention and Problem or, in my words, Intention and Counter-Intention go hand in hand. They are two sides of the same coin. Deal with goals and you also have to deal with everything that is between you and the goal. That is the nature of physical reality and there is no way around this as long as you live on Planet Earth. Why do I say "Counter-Intention" rather than Objection? Because whatever the Objection or the Problem is, is an Intention too. You may not be consciously aware that it is your intention not to have money, but as long as you maintain half-conscious or subconscious focus on not-having-money it is an Intention and some reason you are holding on to not-having money. By calling your doubts Counter-Intentions we acknowledge our own responsibility for having these doubts, we acknowledge that they are not just some mysterious doubt that arises out of nowhere to harass you, but they are things you must have unwittingly put in place yourself or bought into somewhere along the way. In practical terms for using the technique, counter-intentions are whatever thoughts spontaneously come up after you voice your intention.

Some examples for Counter-Intentions of the statement "I allow myself to have $15 000 Dollars a month with ease"

I can't do it with ease, it will take hard work

I can't just have something from nothing

I don't deserve that much

How am I supposed to achieve that?

From where is it supposed to come?

Oh, how I wish that were true.

We'll see

Maybe some day

There is no telling whether I will ever make that kind of money

I just don't know how

Should I change my job?

Should I seek legal advice?

Some examples for lower-level counter-Intentions that might come up when you're in even worse shape mentally and emotionally:

This stuff wont work

I'm afraid of loosing it all

I've tried similar techniques before, they have never worked – ever.

I have a headache

I feel so fucking exhausted

I give up

Some examples for higher-level counter-Intentions that might come up on better days and deceive you into thinking you've "got it":

That would be great

Even $5000 I could accept

I'm feeling hopeful already

Wow, wow, wow – that would be amazing!

Even though thoughts like these indicate that you are getting closer to manifestation, that you are currently in a better mood, in using RCT (Reality Creation Technique) they are also handled as counter-intentions because they do not match the original Intention. If the original Intention was $15 000, then even the real manifestation of $5000 is a counter-intention.

In short: Everything other than the real-life, physical manifestation of your Intention is a counter-Intention. What if it doesn't manifest? Well, it not manifesting is the counter-intention. And what if, after handling the counter-intention, it still doesn't manifest? Well, it still not manifesting **is** the counter-intention. The question is never whether something works or not, whether something manifests or not but if **you** are **wiling** to focus **until** it manifests. That is the awesome and extremely powerful philosophy behind RCT.

The Basic Technique

I just gave you examples of counter-intentions. But listing them, like I just did, is not done in RCT Sessions. In Session, you have to keep a balance of placing the focus on your Intention and placing the Focus on Counter-Intentions. I wrote down one intention and twenty-three counter-intentions. That is imbalanced. Actually per one voicing of an intention, only one counter-intention is to be handled. So a basic RCT Session would actually sound something like this:

"I allow myself to have $15 000 Dollars a month with ease"

"I honestly don't know whether that's true or not."

"I allow myself to have $15 000 Dollars a month with ease"

"Yeah right, dream on"

"I allow myself to have $15 000 Dollars a month with ease"

"I can accept the amount, but I can't accept the with-ease part"

"I allow myself to have $15 000 Dollars a month with ease"

"What does "with ease" mean anyway?."

"I allow myself to have $15 000 Dollars a month with ease"

"Again, I just don't know if that's true."

"I allow myself to have $15 000 Dollars a month with ease"

"Same objection, I just don't know if that's true."

"I allow myself to have $15 000 Dollars a month with ease"

"There is no way of knowing that for certain."

This is a more proper use of the RCT because focus on the counter-intention does not take a priority to the Intention. On planet Earth it is actually quite common to focus much more attention on the unwanted than the wanted, so the RCT will gradually reduce that conditioned behaviour.

You now do have the outline of the basic-version of the technique. I know you are eager to get started but do read on before you start because there are several add-ons to the technique to make it deeper, longer-lasting and more effective.

When and How to Use it

Ideally you do not use this technique while doing something else. People think "Alright, I'll do this while washing the dishes" or "I'll do this when driving the car" or "I'll combine this with Workout". If these realities you'd like to create are really important to you, you will treat them with enough respect to reserve time, attention and space just for them and them only. Otherwise your Intention becomes nothing more than a shallow, repetitive recording. I also recommend not to repeat the Intention again and again and again in one piece but to distribute your session over an entire day. So if you repeat it 20 times a day it is better to do that at different times of the day then all 20 at once. Do it only once, twice, three times and at the very most five times. Then take a break and do one or a few more later. Then take a break and just live life and do a few more later. Also, do not do more than 50 repetitions a day. Personally, when I have an Intention I repeat it about 20 times a day. There are several reasons for all of this:

The advantages of repeating your Intention every day, again and again and again and again is that your body-mind familiarizes itself with the energy-vibration of the preferred reality. The disadvantage of frequent repetition is that it can become shallow, boring, insincere, automatic or non-wholehearted. It then becomes like normal affirmations (which don't work precisely because of the shallowness) where someone says one sentence over and over again without feeling much. Or even worse, it becomes like those audio-recordings which make certain statements over and over but they don't really mean much to the person. Or worse still, so called "subliminal affirmations" where one does not even consciously know what is being intended. As many readers of this booklet will already have experienced, the effectiveness of such methods is limited – not to mention that there is not much joy or life-experience to be gained from them or from trying to avoid any effort at all.

The only exception to this rule is if you are an advanced practitioner of RCT and are willing to work with whatever comes up consciously and with full care and sincerity. In that case you can occasionally allow yourself to do a session for several hours. My own longest session was for several days. That's right, I worked the intention and counter-intentions all the time, only taking breaks for eating, sleeping, restroom and occasional short breaks. I was dealing with a pressure in my forehead that I had had since childhood and I wanted healing from and it took a full 4 days of RCT – that's some pretty hardcore determination! – to heal it (that was 14 years ago and it hasn't come back since). But as long as you're in Beginners mode its best to not get into too much wilfulness and allow for some resting and some manifestation-work by higher forces than yourself. So you'd limit your session to five repetitions and then go about your day only to return to full awareness of your Intention later in the day. This is good because daily life often tends to take people out of awareness of their Intention, out of Alignment with their Intention. So going back to it more than once a day is a must when using RCT.

Handling Counter-Intentions

After voicing the intention, notice what comes up **spontaneously**. In RCT we only handle that which comes up spontaneously as a counter-intention. Why?

Because otherwise RCT turns into a witch-hunt for negativity and hidden programs and subconscious-beliefs. And guess what you'll get if you keep looking for problems and counter-intentions? That's right, you'll get more of them. The truth is that there is no limit to the counter-intentions and doubts available in mass-consciousness because there are no limits to the thoughts that the Universe creates. You could literally go on for decades "handling counter-intentions" if you address every single on. The purpose of RCT is not to "handle all doubts" or "dissolve all problems". That's where many practitioners of reality-creation techniques get lost. The purpose is to have at least enough control over your attention so that it is aware of or focussed on the preferred reality at least 51% of the time. 51% is quite enough to have it manifest. That means you can have it manifest despite doubts, you can have it despite issues and problems and challenges and blocks. Some schools teach that you can't have it unless *all* issues are solved – this rigid way of seeing things can actually stop manifestation. So your Intention is complete when counter-intentions don't come up spontaneously, when they don't force themselves into your field of perception, when you'd have to purposefully look for them in order to find them. When no more counter-intentions come up in this way and you feel the reality of your Intention 100% or it manifests right there on the spot, then that Intention-Cycle is completed and you can take a break and enjoy your new reality or move on to new Intentions.

There are hundreds of different ways of handling counter-intentions but I strongly recommend, from 15 years of experience with RCT, you only work with the ones presented in this book.

Releasing Resistance

First of all, plenty of counter-intentions dissolve or loose energy-charge merely by you noticing them. That's because many of these thought-patterns only have power and momentum because you are not quite aware of them operating. To use a modern example, this would be similar to you not being quite aware of how Google works and therefore not only being in awe or even fear of Googles power but also totally unaware of when a Business competitor uses Google to your disadvantage. Some problems and thought-patterns that come up require more than mere noticing, they require acknowledgement. That is the opposite of resistance or trying to ignore or push away an issue. Acknowledgement is like saying "Hello" and accepting that something is there. Resistance will only strengthen the problem. A part of releasing counter-intentions is releasing your resistance towards them. That is a must in RCT, there is no way around that. To heighten your understanding of why, imagine your hand pushing against a wall. Or even right now, push your hand against a wall. Where is your attention? Where is your energy going? That's right, to the wall. So by resisting problems you are actually fuelling them with energy. By trying to push away problems you are actually holding them in mind. To quit energizing problems, stop resisting them. That is an Art you will train yourself to learn throughout using RCT. RCT not only spouts Intentions as

"Affirmations" but also includes counter-intentions and objections for the very reason that suppressing negativity only increases it. In fact, suppressing or trying to avoid problems is not a sign of positivity or spiritual awareness, but a sign of cowardice. You are big enough to confront every issue, you are strong enough to handle issues. These issues do not arise "because of" the RCT – they are issues that are *already* within you and your energy-field. And here's news for you: You ought to be happy that they come up because they are precisely the hurdles that need to be crossed in order to achieve the goal. If your goal is the top of the mountain, you'd enjoy the path to it, you'd enjoy the tree logs and rocks and animals in your way because that would mean that you are on your path that you really did get on your way to the goal. If nothing comes up and no problem arises to overcome, you are not getting closer to your goal. Get it? "Problems" should therefore be not only not resisted but much more than that, they should be embraced, enjoyed, celebrated. You take the Bull by the horns and it will ride you straight to your goal.

Enjoy the "Problem" as a Stepping-Stone to Manifestation

So it is of crucial importance to begin to enjoy the objections, blocks, challenges, counter-intentions that present themselves, to appreciate them as the very stepping stones to the full manifestation of your Intention. Once you quit responding to them like some kind of wuss and instead react to them like someone tough enough to handle it and free and powerful enough to overcome even that, these blocks will disappear.

Sources of Counter-Intentions

We've seen how RCT is done in writing but more often you will be doing it verbally. You will voice the intention. Then you look at what comes up. Then, as best you can, you express that in words. A counter-intention does not always have to be a thought or a word, in which case you simply mimic whatever comes up. It can be

A feeling

An emotion

Tiredness

An intuition

A thought

A memory

A fantasy

A physical sensation

An inner aversion or resistance

A contraction

An energy in your stomach, solar-plexus, chest, forehead or crown

An urge to do something else

And it can come from any level-of-emotion or level-of-energy. It can come from the lowest ebbs of shame, guilt, apathy, grief, fear, anger. It can come from the mid-ranges of frustration, doubt, pride, boredom. It can come from higher-levels such as courage, neutrality and joy. Often an Intention does manifest when you have moved up to the level of joy on the subject. So when you voice it and you feel joy about it, which is an indicator that it is already on its way. But if your Intention does not manifest, despite the joy, then the joy becomes the counter-intention and can be released as such.

Mimicking

If you wish to go beyond the mere noticing and voicing of the counter-intention, mimicking is a good method for that. It is slightly more advanced and you can build it in once in awhile. Mimicking undoes resistance because it builds an element of Humor and Lightness to your RCT Practice. Seriousness is an indicator of inner resistance − resistance toward a counter-intention, resistance toward the intention (yes, humans subtly resist even their own Intentions) or resistance toward the RCT exercise. Every time you are too serious you know you are bottling up Emotions that want to flow up and out. In any case Mimicking means you are copying the thought or counter-intention but not in a way that takes it too seriously but in a way that is imitating the mind or imitating the problem and even **mocking** the problem. Many people who I have taught RCT discontinue for the sole reason that they start taking the unwanted more serious than the Intention. Doing this eventually has the counter-intention win. So watch out not buy into the convincing victim-act of the mind and all of its "problems". In very intense variations of RCT the mimicking can take on the tone of an actor exaggerating the problem or thought in quick succession with voicing the Intention. This can have some hilarious effects while at the same time freeing long-held energy. It is not possible to demonstrate this on this piece of paper so I do recommend you listen to the *Reality Creation Technique Audio* which is available at www.realitycreation.net I've recorded the audio to demonstrate what the various RCT Variations sound like in real life.

Alternating

The alternating-technique means that you stick to one counter-intention and repeatedly alter it with your intention until the objection looses all meaning or sounds silly. This may be necessary sometimes with persistent counter-intentions that keep coming up. That would look something like this:

"I allow myself to have $15 000 Dollars a month with ease"

"That's too good to be true"

"I allow myself to have $15 000 Dollars a month with ease"

"Nope, That's too good to be true"

"I allow myself to have $15 000 Dollars a month with ease"

"That's just too damn good to be true!"

"I allow myself to have $15 000 Dollars a month with ease"

"That's too good to be true"

"I allow myself to have $15 000 Dollars a month with ease"

"That's too good to be true"

"I allow myself to have $15 000 Dollars a month with ease"

"Sorry, but that's too good to be true"

"I allow myself to have $15 000 Dollars a month with ease"

"That's too good to be true"

"I allow myself to have $15 000 Dollars a month with ease"

"That's too good to be true"

Only when the counter-intention is "flat" would you move on with the process. Of Course this is not for beginners because beginners should not be doing more than five voicings of the Intention and Counter-Intention a piece anyway. Later, after you've actually manifested a thing or two you may acquaint yourself with the advanced practice of mimicking, alternating and even mixing all practices.

Emotional Releasing

This is an alternative way of handling counter-intentions and it may work better for some people. After voicing your intention, check whether there is a tightness, contraction, heaviness or uneasiness in one of your energy-centers which are traditionally:

Stomach

Solar-Plexus

Chest

Forehead

Crown

These are the places where stuck energy is felt most clearly. Of course it might also be elsewhere such as in the throat, leg, neck, shoulders, mouth or one might even feel an energy-field surrounding the body. But for beginners these energy-centers will suffice. Assuming there must be more to it somewhere unseen is merely creating more problems to solve. Any type of stuckness or counter-intention you have also exists as a stuck energy in one of the energy-centers. So get in touch with that contraction or tension and let it come up and out. Synonyms and Alternatives (so that you really "get" what I'm talking about here):

Open Up

Allow it to Flow

Allow it to Be

Allow it to Pass Through

Give Up Resisting it

Give up wanting to Change it

Open a Window in that Area

Breathe with it

Stick an imaginary tube into it and let the energy flow out

Go to the center of it

Allow it to dissolve

Welcome it

Welcome all sensations, feelings, memories and thoughts that come up with it

Just feel it

Relax with it

Be with it

Let it go

One of these or a combination of these will dissolve the energy. Its actually not really the energy that dissolves but only the resistance – by which fear or anger or sadness no longer feel like fear, anger or sadness but like warmth, relaxation or even joy.

If you require practice learning how to Release, try out "Ultimate Release", "Emotional Clearing" or similar at www.realitycreation.net or check out the Infinity Course at www.infinitycourse.com

Because this may take a little longer than normal handling of counter-intentions you may repeat the Intention 2-5 times before doing another round of releasing. So that would be:

"I enjoy a wonderful relationship with a partner that is just right for me"

Emotional Releasing

"I enjoy a wonderful relationship with a partner that is just right for me"

"I enjoy a wonderful relationship with a partner that is just right for me"

"I enjoy a wonderful relationship with a partner that is just right for me"

Emotional Releasing

"I enjoy a wonderful relationship with a partner that is just right for me"

"I enjoy a wonderful relationship with a partner that is just right for me"

"I enjoy a wonderful relationship with a partner that is just right for me"

"I enjoy a wonderful relationship with a partner that is just right for me"

"I enjoy a wonderful relationship with a partner that is just right for me"

Emotional Releasing

This is continued until you feel free regarding the subject or it manifests. This can take a few hours but it can also take several months. It happens when its ready to happen. Pushing it is only a sign of Resistance. Give up pushing, let the Universe manage it.

As a rule, RCT should not only be done with voicing intentions and counter-intentions. You should be doing some emotional releasing as well once in awhile. Otherwise you will eventually get stuck on one emotional level without moving up. As you release emotions you release energy and your life changes according to the energy you radiate. Eventually the type of Intentions you have also changes.

So while Intention/Counter-Intention-Voicing is the Basic Technique it should be intensified by Intention/Counter-Intention-Emotional-Releasing and also by the following Intention/Counter-Intention-Deeper-Releasing. It is up to you how often you add

Emotional Releasing to the process but I recommend you do it but I usually add at least one session a day.

Sometimes contractions in your solar-plexus, chest or stomach do not come up during the RCT Session but somewhere or suddenly throughout the day. In this case it is recommended that you take a break from whatever you were doing and attend to the emotional counter-intention that is now **offering** itself to you for processing.

Deeper Releasing

Deeper Releasing categorizes the nature of the Counter-Intentions by their origin. Whatever the mind can categorize it has an easier time letting go of. The origin of all intentions and counter-intentions is **Desire and Resistance**.

Other words for Desire:

Want

Long For

Crave

Need

Wish

Other words for Resistance:

Aversion

Push away

Not-Wanting

Saying No-To

Avoidance

Fighting

Desire keeps us separate from our preferred reality because it implies "not having", it implies lack. This is actually contrary to what you mistakenly learn in 80% of all self-improvement and metaphysical literature on the subject. Desire is not creative. In order to have an Intention there was probably first a Desire for something. But if you stop at the Desire you will create only lack and more lack. Your native state is actually **Infinite** and every Desire implies that you are separate from all-that-is, separate from the natural and vast abundance of the Universe. It's a moot point to as what was there first – the lack, or the Desire. Suffice it to say that both go hand in hand and you can start getting used to moving from Desire to Belief, from mere Wanting to Having, from mere Wishing to Deciding. Resistance on the other hand, "paradoxically" brings the things we do not want closer to us. And that is the comedy of life: Everything we want stays away and everything we don't want comes to us. For people who do not understand how energy operates, life can become quite a nightmare. Everything you say "Yes" to, you activate and everything you say "No" to, you also activate. There is no difference between "Yes" and "No" because Infinity is non-dual, is One. Resistance is saying "No". Desire is saying "Yes" but its saying yes to "I don't have it". Intention is saying "Yes" to the reality you prefer.

All issues, emotions and counter-intentions can be traced back to a collection of wants and resistances which are:

Wanting **Love**/Attention/Approval (Resisting Disapproval/Criticism)

Wanting **Control**/Power – (Resisting Powerlessness)

Wanting **Freedom**/Separation/Superiority (Resisting Unity/Inferiority/Emprisonment)

Wanting **Unity**/Oneness (Resisting Separation/Freedom)

Wanting **Safety**/Security/Certainty (Resisting Uncertainty/The Unknown)

Again, you can trace all issues to one of these 5 items. All issues are only five items. If you don't believe it, check for yourself. What are some issues you are having? And which one of these do they come from? In every single case you will find the thought or emotion or problem coming from the **want** of one of these. Just to make sure there is no misunderstanding here: Having Love, Control, Freedom, Unity and Safety are not the problem. The problem is wanting them, which translates as lacking them.

As an RCT student you are asked to learn these 5 items by heart so that you can trace any intention or counter-intention back to one of them.

Here's a transcript of a coaching-session so that you can see how the technique is used. I'm also going to show some non-conventional variations and uses of the technique because my coaching-sessions are never statically fixed to doing the method in one way. They are flexible and malleable according to what comes up. The technique is only the basic framework, the context.

Coach: Intention?

Student: I am a humorous, happy and energetic person

Coach: Counter? (In coaching-sessions I don't use the full wording)

Student: Actually I'm fatigued most of the time

Coach: Can you feel that fatigue right now?

Student: A little

Coach: OK; so allow yourself to feel it.

Student: OK

Coach: …

Coach: Is that coming from wanting Love, Control, Freedom, Unity or Safety?

Student: (checks to see which want it is coming from)

Student: Wanting Freedom. Feeling imprisoned by heaviness and wanting Freedom.

Coach: OK, notice the wanting-freedom a little more. Welcome it.

Student: …

Coach: Could you release your attention from wanting freedom? Could you just relax now?

Student: OK

Coach: Intention.

Student: I am a humorous, happy and energetic person

Coach: Any objection? (I sometimes use this instead of "Counter?")

Student: Its still the fatigue a little.

Coach: Feel the fatigue. Could you just allow it to be there? Give yourself permission to feel a little tired? Do you love and respect yourself enough to give yourself some rest and space to have that feeling?

Student: Yeah, alright (student relaxes visibly)

Coach: Intention.

Student: I am a humorous, happy and energetic person.

Coach: Intention. (When not spoken clearly or with confidence or in order to strengthen someone's focus on the Intention, I sometimes have them repeat the Intention once or twice before moving on)

Student: I am a humorous, happy and energetic person

Coach: Counter-Intention?

Student: I don't know.

Student: That is, I don't know if I will be humorous. I'm always so serious.

Coach: Does being serious come from wanting Approval, Control, Freedom, Unity or Safety?

Student: …

Student: Approval. It comes from wanting Approval. Being afraid to be rejected.

Coach: Feel that lack of Approval. Give yourself some time and allow the Emotion to come up.

Student:…

Coach: Allow it some more.

Student:…

Coach: Could you, for now, let go of being needy of approval? Could you just rest?

Student: Yeah.

Coach: Intention.

Student: I am a humorous, happy and energetic person.

Coach: What do you think about that? (yet another variation to ask for counter-intentions)

Student: Well, its certainly a nice idea.

Coach: OK.

Coach: Intention.

Student: I am a humorous, happy and energetic person.

Coach: Any doubts?

Student: Not so much anymore. Its more of a looking forward to my new life as a joker. (Laughs)

Coach: Is that coming from wanting Attention, Control, Security, Freedom or Unity?

Student: Unity. Togetherness with others.

Coach: Alright. For now, let go of needing Togetherness with others.

Student: OK.

Coach: And allow yourself to remember and feel the Togetherness you already have with people.

Student: OK

Coach: Intention?

Student: I am a humorous, happy and energetic person.

Coach: Counter?

Student: The question "What is happiness?" arises

Coach: Could you let go of that question?

Student: No.

Coach: Could you hold on to it?

Student: Yes. (Laughs). Nevermind.

Coach: Intention.

Student: am a humorous, happy and energetic person.

This particular session went on for several hours and many, many, many more counter-intentions until the student finally gave in to his new reality. He ended by saying "I could have had this great feeling hours ago if only Id made the final decision to have this reality".

Coaching-Sessions can go longer than I previously recommended because I'm a Pro in dealing with RCT. If you are alone I do not recommend you go even as long as transcribed to on these pages. Why? Because of the state of overwhelm and "getting lost" that the mind sometimes reacts with when Intentions keep getting repeated. Your body/mind and energy-field have enough to handle by doing only your 2-5 repetitions per Session, not to mention more.

I recommend you apply "Deeper Releasing" to your Intentions at least once a week if not more often. I also recommend you apply it to your Intention at least once or twice. If they really are your Intentions, this will tend to strengthen them because you are not releasing the Intention but merely the wants (=lacks) behind it. So if your intention is "I allow myself to have $15 000 Dollars a month with ease", then ask yourself whether that is coming from wanting Freedom, Control, Security, Love, Unity. If you see it coming from all five then only look at one at a time. If its coming from a needing security, feel that for a few seconds and then, as best you can, relax and release your attention from needing security and allow yourself to feel what it would feel like to already have security. If its coming from a needing freedom, feel that for a few seconds and then, as best you can, relax and release your attention from needing freedom and allow yourself to feel what it would feel like to already be free.

Mental RCT

We've looked at RCT in writing and Verbal RCT, which is the most common variation. The same thing can be done mentally by alternating back and forth between your preferred reality and counter-intentions mentally. In The Infinity Course Level 2 I call this "Duality Surfing". So you'd visualize the fulfilment of your Intention, then you'd shift your attention to an objection and you'd go back and forth again and again, until

    a)   shifting back and forth is no longer a problem

b) there is no resistance toward the negative or opposite side

c) there is no resistance toward the positive side or what you intend

d) you can easily put your attention on the preferred reality and feel it as real

Of course you are also permitted to combine written, verbal and mental RCT. While voicing your Intention you may also sometimes want to visualize it or see it in your minds eye. It is no *must* to visualize it, but it is permitted.

Action RCT

The technique can also be carried out in the Form of physical action. Throughout life what you are doing is either in alignment with your Intentions or it isn't. There are no "good" or "bad" actions except in relation to your Intentions. So if relaxation is your Intention, then lying around is no counter-action to that. If working all day is your Intention than lying around suddenly becomes a counter-action. Simply put, all actions that are contrary to your intention are the demonstration or display of counter-intentions. It is through your physical actions and behaviour that you demonstrate what your true Intentions and Beliefs are. There are only three types of actions that are not counter-intentive:

- Actions that allow for more creativity, self-expression, responsibility, courage, joy, love or peace.

- Action-steps that are done toward the goal

- Actions where you behave or act **as if** you have reached the goal

If your Intention is "I allow myself to have $15 000 Dollars a month **with ease**" then very hard work would actually be a counter-intention. If however the goal is "I allow myself to have $15 000 Dollars a month" hard work is in alignment with that Intention.

Examples for "Acting-As-If" in regards to the Intention "I allow myself to have $15 000 Dollars a month"

- Test-driving a new car

- Saying "no" to an unfriendly customer

- Spending a day at a Spa as if you had no worries in the world

- Having time for creative projects because you "already have enough money"

As-if actions are actually even more powerful than actions-toward-the-goal because they produce an energy-field of already having as opposed to wanting. You always receive back in life what you feel you already have. (More on the as-if method in my book "Parallel Universes of Self")

Many people interested in creating reality, the new thought movement, "the law of attraction" ask me whether action is necessary to fulfil a preferred reality. So here's a little inside-secret I have to share:

Many people who are attracted to reality-creation-literature and courses have an **aversion towards physical-reality.** They'd like to have some magic Formula fix it for them rather than actually deal with their goals, dreams and intentions and all the hurdles and issues that brings up. Along with this exhaustion with life (which they usually hide from themselves) comes an aversion against physical action, which is labelled as "laziness". Action or Working is perceived as "difficult". In reality, and successful people know this, action is fun. Physical life on earth is fun. We embrace physical reality, we embrace action, we embrace work. What purpose would it have to incarnate as physical beings and then not want to participate in physicality? What point is it to long for the soul-realm when you previously really looked forward to trying out the physical realm? Generally speaking I recommend all readers of this to soften their resistance of action and work and challenges.

Having said that, yes, it is possible to manifest realities without action or work. That sounds crazy to conventional science, but its one of the whole points of using things such as "The Reality Creation Technique". The amount of focus required to create a new reality depends on the level of Energy you are experiencing the world from. Using a scale from 1 to 1000...

Below 200 you don't have the energy to create a new reality. You're in reactive mode, a victim of the circumstances. Surroundings and others dictate what happens.

From 200-300 creating a new reality requires a lot of effort and a lot of work. Get off your lazy ass and do something.

From 300-400 you realize that if your thoughts and emotions are in alignment with your Intentions, work is required, but less of it. You first align your energy, and then you act. In this way your actions bear more fruits.

From 400-500 you realize that some things happen by thought, word and feeling alone. You need a lot of repetition and practice for it to happen, but happen it does.

From 500-600 you realize that all it needs is your Intention or Decision and it is so.

Above 600 you are no longer interested in manifesting Intentions.

(For more Info on the Levels of Energy, see my book of the same title)

What is generally true for the RCT Practitioner is:

It is important to me that my Intention manifests, no matter if by thought, word, deed or all three.

If it is your aim to release all of your resistances in life (and it should be if you understand anything about Reality Creation), then it doesn't matter whether you have to act or not. You'll be more than happy to act. Productivity and Creativity are sure signs that you're in flow. Being in flow means to be in alignment with your Intentions.

So go ahead and do, act, work. Just make sure that before you do so, you feel well, you feel at ease, you feel joyful about your Intentions and your life. Otherwise your actions will be "compensation actions" meant to make-up for negative creating. And that type of work and action is certainly a waste of energy. An example for compensation action: Lets say you go to evening school for a year because you are afraid of not getting the right jobs. You have wasted a lot of time because you could have simply intended that you have a good job and then invest your time into actions toward that goal instead of toward what you are afraid of. Another example: You workout 2 hours a day because you feel inadequate compared to others. 2 hours is a lot. You could have saved time by releasing your feelings of inadequacy first. No amount of workout will release those feelings properly. So the rule of the thumb is always: First get into a good state, then act. Otherwise all of your actions will be coloured negatively, will be inspired by lack and create more lack. When, on the other hand, your actions are inspired by joy, they will lead to more joy.

Escapes

Some of the things we use to avoid feeling/releasing or avoid going for our goals; some of the counter-intentional actions we as modern day humans regularly do are:

Internet

Email

Television

Telephoning

Gaming

Chit-Chatting

Watching Movies

Listening to Music

Seeing Friends

Going Out

Eating

Sleeping

Taking Drugs (including Alcohol and Tobacco)

There is nothing wrong with these actions in and of themselves. They become an issue when we do them *coming from* a feeling of lack instead of fullness. Did you know that coffee tastes much better coming from joy than coming from a need to feel-better or wake-up? It's the same with all other things. Going through life in Resistance and Unawareness leads to Exhaustion and Energylessness. Exhaustion then leads to wanting to "Escape it all" by just flopping down on the coach and going Online pointlessly or watching TV or doing one of the many other things we do to cover-up resistance. Especially doing them way too long, beyond the call for mere relaxation or temporary distraction makes them counter-intentional. When someone spends all day at work and all evening at home in front of the Internet you can be certain they have some intense emotional issues they are running away from. The funny thing is that you cannot really escape the energy / emotion you are carrying around with you. Sooner or later it will come up again and needs to be addressed and processed in order to dissolve for good.

Everything that happens relates to your Intentions

Nothing happens outside of your Intention. As an RCT Practitioner you know there is no such thing as an "outside of or beside the exercise". Everything is the exercise and your entire day reflects who you are regarding your Intentions. Everything that happens has something to do with the Intentions you are working on. Everything that happens has something to do with the predominant energy-vibration you are radiating. You cannot experience any differently than you radiate. In this way you do have control over what happens and does not happen.

Don't make it happen, allow it to happen

Its not actually you creating, it's the energy field some call "The Universe". The Universe is able to provide everything as evidenced by all the bodies, trees, mountains, planets, stars its created.

Use it until it works

Use the Reality Creation Technique until it works, no matter how long it takes. There are few things more fulfilling than seeing the power of your word manifest.

CHAPTER TWO

REALITY CREATION BY DIVINE WILL

The Reality Creation Technique is a method of bringing things about by personal will, by intense and repeated focus. The methods of reality creating presented in this chapter are different. They apply a softer touch and a "giving it to the Universe" attitude. Both paths – the path of personal will and the path of Divine Will – should be learned by a Reality Creation Practitioner.

The Stream of Life

Life is a stream that always flows whether you like it or not. Resist the flow and it overwhelms you. Swim with it and you can use it to your advantage. It was already flowing when you arrived to it and it will always reach the destination it is meant to reach. The Stream diverges from and converges into several different streams, each of them representing a different reality.

You are sitting in a boat that is floating with the stream. You have been given oars to paddle. With these oars you can try to go against the stream or paddle quicker with the stream. None of these two are necessary to reach the destination that is perfect and natural for you. Merely and merrily sitting in the boat will be enough for you to arrive exactly where life has ordained.

Paddling against the stream (going upstream) is what most call „life". This type of struggle is a waste of energy and does not lead you to your most ideal and natural destination. Instead it slows your progress. If it has any benefit at all, then that is that it makes you stronger. The only reason someone would paddle upstream is because he does not trust that the river is taking him to the right places speedily and efficiently. He has lost his basic *trust* in life, the universe, God and feels the need to paddle elsewhere. Another reason for paddling upstream could be because he was taught that resistance will solve problems. He will exert himself until he becomes so exhausted he gives in to the natural stream again. Many believe that where the stream is taking them is not to their liking and that life must be a fight. But most are somewhere in between. While they go with the flow sometimes, they put on a lot of brakes with their oars because they don't want to go too fast. Going too fast they think they'd be unable to enjoy their current surroundings or that they would crash into a rock sticking out of the water.

Going with the stream does not necessarily mean going with the *mainstream,* with the stream everyone else is going. There are many streams and many other side streams of side-streams which diverge from and converge into each other. Going with the stream (downstream) means „teaming up"with a life force that is more powerful and efficient than what you could do on your own. It means to make use of the strong current *already there, already available, already accessible.*

From where you stand as the "normal human being" there are various alternatives to the half-crazed and hysterical upstream paddling widely practiced. People who use these "alternatives" (which are not really *alternative* but actually normal), are called "wizards", "magic people", "powerful people". This is rather funny because its actually the other way around. Those who go with the stream are actually those who are behaving *naturally*. Those who experience "miracle" after miracle are actually experiencing a normal part of life, while those who try paddling or even swimming upstream all the time are actually abnormal. One could go as far as to say that it is *they* who are the wizards because they are expending an unbelievable amount of energy.

Leading a good and successful life takes some discipline and effort in terms of focusing, in terms of bringing the boat into alignment with the stream, but this is not the type of effort society thinks is required. You don't have to deserve success, make it, reach it, fulfil it, achieve it, create it. It is a given. A birthright. Normal. It actually happens by itself when you are your most natural self. You don't believe that? Then you are one of the crazies. But that's forgiven, most people are.

You have been taught that "your action is what moves mountains". Contrast this belief by looking around you. Look at the trees. The stars. The mountains. Look at whatever you see outside of your window. The sun. The grass. The leaves. The sand.

Has any of this come about by *you*? Or is it much more a result of life itself, of some divine force?

Take a minute to look around at all the things that *already exist* without you having needed to do anything.

Will you admit that almost everything that exists and is happening, just happened, without any deliberate involvement or work required from you?

Face the obvious. If I asked you to „create a plant" would you start trying to glue and paste sticks and leaves together or simply put a seed into the ground and let the *force* take care of it? There is some type of *force* creating all of this, isn't there? It doesn't matter if you view it scientifically (evolution, big bang) or religiously (God) or spiritually (the universe, the field). You can witness a *force* creating all manners of things with ease, beauty and elegance. How much effort would you have to invest in order to achieve only one single structure that this *force* produces by the trillions? Do you see how it is not your job to create the stream but only to *choose* a stream?

Do you think that if you learned more about this force, more about this *source* that would be more worthwhile than anything else? Could you then perhaps „team up" with this source/force to have your life run more smoothly and be more fulfilling?

If this source can create entire galaxies it shouldn't have a problem creating the comparatively minor stuff on your personal wish-list, should it?

The "stream" we have been talking about is an energy-stream, not visible with the eyes but feel able with the inner sense. Feeling at ease is an indicator that you are going with the stream. Feeling at dis-ease is an indicator of going against the stream. You can let energy pass through, come and go. But the moment you try to build up a dam or push it, it stays stuck in your own energy-field and body.

Let's now look at the different alternatives you have to the "struggle for survival".

One option would be to let go of your oars. This would mean letting go of all control and resistance. What happens? Your life speeds up and you arrival at right-for-you destinations is quicker. It is not you "making" anything anymore, it is not you "doing" anything "in order to achieve something" anymore, it is full surrender and trust in the life force, in the Divine. On a daily life basis this would mean that you trash your plans, goal-lists, your to-do-lists, quit "trying to get" and generally just look at what feels good and right from *day to day*.

While feeling good you would know that you are flowing downstream (with the stream) and when feeling bad you know that you are paddling upstream again, and so you let go of the oars again (interesting isn't it? You let go of the oars but they are still hanging at the side of the boat, ready to be picked up anytime again! *Nothing* is ever lost). You would not use the feeling bad as a cause to paddle even harder (this is *the* most typical mistake the human makes) but as a cause to re-align with the stream, a cause to relax again.

For some, the thought of complete surrender is frightening. What these people don't understand is the paradox that loss of all control is full control. To the mind this is a contradiction. I will not argue with you here. If allowing yourself to be washed away in a stream of joy, straight to where you belong in the nature of things is too frightening for you, you don't have to let go of the oars entirely. But you could at least loosen your grip on them a little bit, no? You hold them so tight that your knuckles turn white. Wasted energy. Let go of them for a minute. Take a deep breathe and relax.

You see? The oars are still there. Nothing has changed except that you are no longer wasting energy. And as you are lying around somewhere or sitting while reading this, you are not in a wild stream anyway, but floating down a gentle river. You don't have to hold on that tight. If you don't want to let go of the oars and follow the paths of least resistance and highest simplicity (the more simple and native and natural something is the more real and therefore effective it is) then you might at least stop paddling upstream. You don't stand a chance. You think you can beat the flow of things you will be disillusioned. Some people who come to practice "reality creation" in my courses are megalomaniacs who actually think that "reality creation" means getting to your destination despite swimming upstream. Others think it means building new artificial rivers...which might be possible with extreme exertion but is not even necessary to arrive at what you wish for.

Where do the rivers of life open out into? They all flow into the vast ocean. In this analogy that would be the "sea of consciousness" or "ocean of energy", what some mystics call "enlightenment" and what I call "the oceanic states" or "the blue states". But why do some wizards not actively seek out enlightenment? Because they know that's where they come from and that's where they will float back to naturally. This is why I do not teach "ascension" or "enlightenment". Trying to "achieve" these things presupposes separation from that ocean. It presupposes that this is not your native state, not where you come from and not where you are going anyway by setting your compass toward positive energy. To me the countless books and retreats and gurus preaching ascension and enlightenment are almost superfluous. Why strive for something that is going to happen anyway? The only reason millions of people in history have been striving to be elsewhere or something else is out of the presupposition that the way things are, the way this planet was created is somehow "wrong" and that the natural order and harmony of things is somehow "disturbed". There is absolutely nothing "wrong" with this Planet – it is meant to be a little difficult and contrasting so that you can learn to exercise choice between positive energy and not-so-positive energy. Thinking life is "no good" they start struggling upstream again. However, it is not "things" or "the universe" that is at fault. It is one's own view of things and behaviour (trying to swim upstream in order to arrive at some goal) that feels bad. And thank goodness this behaviour is designed to feel bad...without the bad feeling we wouldn't know wrong from right, life nurturing from life stifling.

What you have been reading up to now is not only some nice story about rivers and boats, it is a metaphor filled with very practical everyday down-to-earth usefulness.

Getting out of the boat to the side of the river and watching the stream go by is like taking a break or meditation. You are watching the stream of life pass-by but not taking part in it. This contemplative mood allows you to consider your trip up to now, to determine which streams you would like to go down next (possibility of divergence). The "observation from outside" allows you to gain perspective rather than be caught up in the automatic mechanism of it all. It also allows you to take the desperately needed break from fighting against the water. When you get back into the stream (finish your Meditation) it is more probable that you will then be flowing with the stream rather than against it. Why? Because you've taken that time out to see in which direction the stream is actually flowing.

The two helpful modes are therefore swimming with the stream or taking a break at the riverside. It is rarely helpful swimming against the stream. And it is not helpful to try to take a short-cut to another stream (reality) by carrying your boat across land. That would be more waste of time and energy. Nevertheless this is exactly how many behave. They just *have to* "get that thing" at once. In their impatience they drag the boat out of the river and try to find that stream on their own. Would they have stayed in the boat they would have come upon a crossing point naturally. And at this crossing point they could decide to switch life-streams, switch realities naturally. Of course we can also see that arriving at a crossroads and *not deciding* will get us stuck in the middle land protruding in front of us. One who has trouble deciding which stream to go down is caught in the illusion that one stream is somehow "worse" than the other. But they are *both* water. They are both life energy. And they will both lead to good destinations provided you are in a positive emotional state. The only path leading to troublesome destinations is navigating from a negative state (leads to bad choices), swimming or rowing backwards (against the stream) – through which you are exhausted and the scenery around you starts looking bleak and dangerous – or leaving the stream into the wilderness without a map. There are a lot of "lost" people wandering around out there. But sooner or later they too will come upon a stream and be given another choice to get back in. So in a sense, not even the two "bad" options are really "bad"...they are simply other experiences. The point of this analogy is not to define what's good or bad, but to tell you: If you are interested,, there's an easier way to go about life. As most souls are not interested in the easier way but more interested in drama and theatrics, the "with the stream" path will give you a sort of "advantage" over your fellow human beings by which you appear "magical" to them. I say this because the mind loves to calculate its "advantages" before actually applying something. The soul couldn't care less about "being better than others". Nevertheless, a life of *flow* does have its incentives for the mind also.

In pondering this analogy there are thousands of things you can derive from it, of which I will only name a few. You can let the waters and winds guide you. If you wish to change stream, only a little bit of steering is necessary. This "little bit of steering" is what I the *reality creation techniques* are for. This is not hard work (unless you've navigated yourself into troublesome areas, by which you will need some hard work to get back on track). It's only an alignment of *attention* and *intention* with preferred streams. Voicing Intentions on a regular basis is actually the process of steering your boat in the general direction you prefer. The "feeling good" exercises within my *reality creation materials* are not to steer but to make sure you are still flowing *with* the stream. Why do I recommend you trash your to-do-lists, goal-lists and weekly-plans and diaries? Because the "goal list" is focused on a stream not present in the here and now. Steering according to another stream would make your navigation look awkward "Goal-lists" are based upon "I have to do X and X and X, and then I can be at that river" (as if you were not already right inside the stream of life). However, as you see in the analogy, you don't have to do anything to continue progressing down the river. You don't have to leave the river or struggle. Same with to-do lists. And diaries address what has happened before you arrived at this point at the river, which is irrelevant to today. In fact, being focused on the past will make your navigation look even more awkward If you are at a relaxed and silent part of the river and you are steering as if you were in the rocky area you were a month ago, this slows your progress and can even make your boat keel over.

The prime block to progress is making all of this too complicated and assigning too much *importance* to certain things. Assigning too much significance to various events such as rocks protruding from the water or events at the riverside, diverts your attention and makes calm navigation along the stream difficult. Assign too much importance / relevance to something negative and you feel yourself tense up and navigate improperly. Assign too much importance / relevance to something positive and the same thing happens. You become tense and unable to act. A beautiful mermaid pops up out of the river in the near distance. Beautiful yes, enjoyable yes. But if your importance-label is too strong you will loose your calm and attention and cause a boat wreck. Same thing for an ugly alligator swimming through the river. It is the assignment-of-importance towards that alligator that focuses you on it. So instead of steering clear of the alligator you move towards it. That's just the opposite of what you wanted! But you cant stop thinking of that alligator over there. You resist it, fight it...and all the while you move closer.

It is therefore wise to "manage your importances" or the *meaning* you give certain things.

The wizards attitude is: If there is something on your trip along the stream of life that is not to your liking...it is very unimportant. Not significant. Not relevant to who you are. You see, you are not suppressing or ignoring it. You are simply not giving it any power over you. Yes..there´s an alligator swimming over there. B*ut if I don't give him attention, he will not give me attention.* Deep in your heart you know this to be true. You knew it even better as a child. Remember playing hide-and-seek as a child and not being found by the others once you stopped giving them attention? And if there's something on your trip along the stream of life that is to your liking...it is important. But it is not *very* important. Its only important. If it is *very* important you become slave to it. Maybe we should even drop the word "important" and replace it with the even more neutral "interesting". If you want to *have* something try also being OK *without* it. This type of non-neediness will make it so much easier to have it. You also know this to be true, perhaps from flirt-situations with the preferred sex. I sometimes say to students "I guarantee that you will either get it or not". This is an attitude of non-attachment that does not mean disinterest, it just means that lack-consciousness is reduced.

Assigning too much importance to your desires builds up pressure and expectation...two things that actually separate you from what you want. The reality creator does not wish for, need, crave...the wizard only *intends*. And intending is as easy as taking the tiny action of steering the boat to the left or to the right.

Let me demonstrate this: Please raise your arm up into the air. That was intention. Now sit there and only "wish" to raise your arm up in the air. Or "need" to raise your arm up into the air. Or have the "goal" to raise your arm up into the air. You see? Nothing happens. Pure intention has no expectation attached to it. Has no waiting-for-manifestation attached to it. Has no doubts attached to it. If there are any doubts whatsoever about something, then that something is not an intention but only a wish. A wish has no power. Did you have any "doubts" about raising your arm? Not really. If you had any doubts that you could raise your arm you wouldn't be able to raise it. Doubts only arise when you start wanting things that are not within reach or start focusing on the how, when, where of a "goal". This is why in my previous books I taught to either "begin at the end" (as if the goal where already achieved) or place your intention on closer and more reachable things, or write your intention-lists without any result-expectation whatsoever (in a playful manner). All of this is closer to pure intention.

When you identify with something as if it were already real (a technique described in my book "Parallel Universes of Self") what happens in the context of our river-analogy is: Your body starts making the right moves with the steering device of the boat or the paddles *automatically*. Your conscious mind doesn't really know what's going on or why your hand suddenly twitched which caused the boat to diverge to the left lane and into another river. But it just happened because there is a "pull" to that destination. Why? Because your soul and mind are already at that destination. Its only your physical body that requires a time-span, and it is thus pulled in that general direction. How long will it take to get there? As long as you have already aligned with *fulfilment-within* and are happy with that reality (believe in it), it doesn't really matter how long it will take. Asking "how long will it take" is presupposing that its not already real anyway. Its an expression of distrust towards your inner power and belief. Whatever you dream, it is yours once you claim it (intend it) *within*. And as it is yours to keep forever, it becomes totally irrelevant when it comes, when it happens, how it happens, from where it comes, etc. Instead, enjoy the scenery as you float along the river. The river is taking you there. Feeling the reality of your Intention as if it were already true also causes you to notice things you would not have noticed before. This is why this specific visualization exercise works so rapidly. "Omens" and "signs" and "coincidences" appear, showing you which streams to choose. These "omens" are mostly "omens" of stepping stones towards the final destinations and not indicators of the final destination itself, by the way.

Often there are several stations you arrive at before the intended reality becomes manifest. Its all a matter of how comfortable you are with a chosen reality. Once the chosen reality becomes very comfortable, familiar, known...it can fall right into your lap. My job is to visualize, feel and embody. Life will do the rest. The river will do the rest.

Navigating the stream of life is strictly speaking neither control nor total loss of control. It is soft control. With total control you will not move anywhere on the river but only make your life miserable. With absolutely no control you will move quickly, but there is no telling where you will end up (except that it will not be too bad of a place as all rivers lead to enlightenment). The reality creators way is exercising just *some* control, a soft touch to the general direction of the boat.

The only thing more important than this slight steering is staying in alignment with the stream, floating downstream rather than upstream. The way to do this is to bring yourself back into the flow when you notice you are out of it. What helps you to notice if you are in or out is your *internal navigator.* Emotions, Feelings, State, Mood. The many psychological, spiritual, motivational books that are telling you to "get rid of" a bad feeling or "overcome it" are wrong. Well, not entirely wrong, but they only understand half the equation: The bad feeling is very, very, very, very, very welcome because it is *showing* you that you are out of alignment with the stream and are putting extreme brakes on your path to fulfilment. Without this low-down feeling you'd be even more lost. In other words, you don't want to feel good about jumping into the Alligators throat. So when that fearful or angry or depressed or sad feeling arises it *serves* you as an indicator to remind you to get back into alignment with the ever-flowing stream of goodness. It is an indicator that you have turned your boat around and are now paddling the wrong way. That's why it feels so bad. Extremely bad feelings are an indicator that you are not only paddling against the stream (the stream is essentially positive energy. There is no duality of "bad and good energy, there is only *one* energy and that's the stream) but have gotten caught up in a swamp-like part or a sinister suction-whirl of the river. And, as you know, the more you struggle within that part of the river, *the more it drags you in.* The way to get back to a safe place is either to relax completely or to choose thoughts or intentions or activities or surroundings that *currently feel a little bit better* to you. Bad feeling is an indicator of either some thought or some plan or some surrounding or some person or some intention not being in alignment with the stream (note: also some so-called "positive" thoughts are in misalignment with the stream). The solution is to deliberately find the thought or action or surrounding that feels more authentic and relieving or strengthening.

An example: Does it feel bad to give up a project? If so, either your *thoughts* about giving up the project or the your *planned actions* (giving it up) must be changed. So you'd either not give up the project (and if that feels better you've found re-alignment with the stream) or you'd make a *list of thoughts* that feel better *until* you find one that really does feel right. And if the thought

"Giving up the project will open me up to new possibilities" does not give you relief, continue the list until you find a thought that *does*. Its really as simple as that. Do that and you're back on the stream for awhile. Flow, look, enjoy, navigate...until you come upon the next block causing you to turn your boat in the wrong direction. With some practice, in time, you will no longer be turning your boat around every time something looking slightly troublesome comes up. That's why people start going upstream in the first place: They see rocks coming up in the river. Rather than navigating around the rocks or speeding up to jump over them - with self-confidence and joy! - they turn around. But in full *Self-confidence* and expertise, you see that you will confront the rocks either way...whether you waste energy by going upstream and *then* crash into the rocks or whether you go for them *right now*...and put them behind you. If you go for them right now, you will have the energy to jump over them or navigate around them. From this you can see that Procrastination is mostly useless. Just a little bit of Procrastination may allow you to adjust the angle by which you approach the rock, but anything beyond that little bit is a fear-based waste of time.

Nobody is forcing you too choose extremely fast streams. Nobody is forcing you to put on no paddle brakes on those fast streams. You can choose more calm waters. Following the context of this analogy you can see the danger of going at extreme speeds. Extreme speeds are best left to experts. In other words, if you are a beginner at reality creation and you are visualizing like crazy on a daily basis, your boat speeds up. Not being accustomed with the various parameters of navigation and the life stream you can crash into rock or land. Had you gone a bit slower, the crash wouldn't hurt you. You'd be back into the stream again within minutes. Having gone much too quick, because your ego is impatient to finally "prove" his worth and "get" the money or whatever it is, the crash could injure you and the boat. Or in other words: If your state/mood is level 2, you don't get into a wild level 5 river. Instead you choose a level 3 stream.

So go easy on yourself. Never give anything too much importance (in any case, define your importances yourself) and keep guiding your attention to the beautiful, the true and the simple. The stream analogy does contain everything required for a happy and effective life. But *you* can also extrapolate the metaphor to find out more things, other aspects and even well kept world secrets. A metaphorical story is a tool from which you can gain answers to many different things. That's why I set the template with this stream analogy: So that you can do some further thinking and gain further insights on your own.

Row, row, row your boat gently down the stream.

Merrily, merrily, merrily, merrily, life is just a dream.

Intentions of the Soul

A good analogy for discerning between goals of the soul (which feel better when attained) and goals of the world-self (which never quite fulfil you) is shopping for clothes.

Recall buying clothes that seemed to fit but having quickly lost interest in them when coming home. Somehow you tell yourself you will wear it some day, but it mostly just hangs in your closet. The piece of clothing is just not "really me".

Recall buying something you liked at first sight and then later still wore and still liked, something you were satisfied with for a long time. The piece of clothing is "really me".

"The more real you get, the more unreal things get" was a statement once made by one of the Beatles on their height of fame. Heed those words of wisdom. When you real, authentic, true to yourself, magic begins to happen. If you bought the piece of clothing trying to ape someone (a model, a celebrity, a commercial), or fulfil someones expectations (boss, spouse), then you likely bought something that was not meant for you. Just because that piece looks good on others does not mean that it must look good on you. We live in monkey-see, monkey-do land. But following another persons path will *never* lead to you. So when finding a piece of clothing just like their superstar has and finding that it doesn't fit, they will put themselves down for it and tell themselves they are "not good enough". A person talking like that is deeply immersed in the claws of the world - a slave, far, far away from real-self. The truth is, it's not so much that you are "not good enough" or "too fat" or whatever, but that you are *different* than those you try to be like and only when you desire to be your **unique** self will you attract a quality-of-life you think a superstar might have. Models and Actors smiling down to us from various magazines in their prosperity, health and beauty are not up there because they have followed others, are not up there because they have tried to adapt to an artificial image of what they are "supposed to be" and "supposed to wear". They are up there because they knew how to emphasize their individuality – and by showing the true colors of their soul, they *radiate*. And because they radiate, they attract all sorts of attention. It might seem like they have to adapt to obligations and constraints and be something other than they really are (in fact, many TV Shows and

Magazines try to make us think so), but the opposite is true. They are being "really me". What's more is that they are not seeking approval, attention an interest, but feel they have it – which is why they receive it from the crowds.

That doesn't mean you will become rich and famous if you follow your souls intentions, but it does mean that you will become prosperous, acknowledged, successful and healthy in *your* field. That's what naturally happens when the "higher self" is flowing through you.

The world-mind, through its mass-media outlets, keeps presenting you "special people"...without telling you that there is something *special* about *you* too and that this special-ness is your key to the good life. The message world-mind keeps sending is "They are special, they are special, they are special, you are not". Depriving you of uniqueness you become needy of approval, attention, love, etc.

Recall a time you wandered through town or from shop to shop in a restless, uneasy manner, maybe frustrated that you couldn't find your piece of clothing or couldn't decide which to buy. The fact that you couldn't decide is indicative of *neither decision* being in alignment with your soul. Your minds memory of what is "good clothes" or what is "in" and your "good taste" of clothes were of no assistance. So after a long and troublesome search, perhaps accompanied by fatigue, you finally decide for a piece of clothing – but are still not satisfied. What happened here is that you've spent the afternoon not following the path of your soul, not discerning between artificial/foreign intentions and your souls intentions. But following your souls path is much easier than you think. Much easier than loads of spiritual schools and books teach. The moment you notice that something is becoming too damn serious or complicated, or an upcoming decision you are "supposed to" make is tearing you apart, realize that you have *already* left the stream of life (your souls path) and that anything you *do* from this point on will not have the preferred results. Your action henceforth will only create more trouble. In this state it would be better to stop, take a break, relax.

It's not necessary to analyze the clothing or weighing its pros and cons for hours. *The soul "knows" things long before they are grasped by the mind.* The mind is a reactive robot, a tool of the world and does not have to involve itself in everything, or micro-manage every aspect of your life. You are the Boss. After you take your break you feel again refreshed and ready (this is your most native state). You enter a shop in an easygoing, non-expectant state, just as if you are visiting a place where it is not about *getting something* (Ego, World-Self), but enjoying the scenery or the artwork (Soul, Higher-Self). Do you fall into compulsive thinking when visiting some beautiful show? Probably not. And if you start getting unhappy again, leave, go home. Nobody is forcing you to find that perfect piece of clothing today. When exhausted or unhappy, your channel to the soul is blocked anyway, you there's no use in trying to force it. Allow your soul to choose your clothes, not an exhausted mind.

Upon entering the shop in a light-hearted mood, become aware of what it is you want to buy (Intention).

You don't have to elaborate on the details, just become aware of whether you want a sweater, shoes, jeans, a suit, a coat or whatever else. If it's a shirt you want, you simply *intend* a shirt without superfluous conditions or worries. The soul will find and choose the *exactly* right piece at the exactly right time. You will recognize that it's the right piece, because you will *feel* it, because the piece of clothing radiates something that you like. You don't have to know why you like it. You realize that it's what you want and buy it without much hesitation. You remember this type of situation, don't you? It is not necessary to force yourself to find it either...it was already lying somewhere, waiting. You did not have to "create" it. It was already produced, waiting to be discovered by you. There are many things in your life you don't have to do but that are only *waiting to be discovered by you.* They are already close to you, so wake up and open your eyes. If you're in a Relationship, realize that your Partner is even more beautiful and smart than you know. Let go of trying to understand everything, let go of trying to be so smart, let go of trying to figure everything out, and begin seeing the world and others with the eyes of the soul.

Finding that piece of clothing is easy. This is what it would feel like to spend almost every day of your life living the life of your soul rather than the life forced upon you by the world in order to suck the energy out of you. This is how uncomplicated and easy stuff is. Many of us invest more energy in the well-being of others than in our own well-being. This is done out of an indoctrinated sense of "selflessness" and "compassion". What really happens when you project *pity* on to other people, is that you are loosing your own energy and therefore become just as inept as them...with no ability to help. "Helping" others at the expense of your own energy you neither help yourself nor others. But one way the world tries to lure you into not-being-your-true-self is by calling on you to fulfil other peoples expectations rather than following spirit. This is the source of most of our victim-attitudes. The world attempts to cover the souls intentions with artificial/foreign intentions...so that your energy flows to these systems rather than to yourself.

Surprised? This is nothing. Most people think they are lucky to be working as employees, which is basically nothing other than making money for someone else and following their goals, not yours. What's worse, many would be overjoyed at becoming corporate slaves for someone. "Getting Employment" is one of the most popular goals on earth. If you are an employee and reading this, I don't mean to offend you. If you wish to get out of the 9 to 5 rat race, realize that you *can* create a different life. It is the worlds nature to replace goals that are native to you, with external ones. I suspect that most of the goals you have are not really *your* goals. Think about it.

Let's suppose finding that special piece of clothing takes a long time in coming. Are you starting to doubt it even exists? Are you doubting its on display in some shop, waiting for you to pick it up? That's nonsense. You *know* that it is waiting for you. And if you don't find it in the first shop, you will find it in the tenth. *What difference does it make?* Be light-hearted and happy *before* you find it, happy about just being alive and strolling through downtown, then it won't matter how many shops you have to visit before reaching it. Because it is *yours* it will not run away. And what if someone else buys it although it does not fit to that person? Is it gone then? No. In that case you will find another piece that matches your souls intent. All the efforts you thought you have to go through in order to survive are superfluous. You needn't worry that you have "wasted the day trying to find a piece of clothes" and you needn't be discouraged as if that piece didn't exist. Discerning your clothes from clothes that is not-you is not done by thinking in normal terms of "right" and "wrong" or "advantages and disadvantages" of the piece of clothing. Why? Because there are all kinds of factors, including the sales person in the shop that will try to convince you that something is right-for-you. Or that it's "the last piece of clothing in this style, your last chance to buy!!!!!" – that's Bullshit. The world-mind is full of artificial tension.

The salesperson does not have a clue what is right for your soul (and if he does he is one hell of a heavenly salesperson). The mind does not really know right from wrong either, it's in a kind of Hypnosis most of the time. Kindness to others is foreign to the mind because all of its attention is sucked into "me, me, me". This makes the mind weak and oblivious to what's actually going on. You won't be able to stop the mind, so just allow it to ramble on. It has nothing to do with you. Allow it to ponder the Pros and Cons of purchasing the piece of clothing, allow it to ponder the risks, while being pressured by the salesperson. Steeped in self-importance the mind hardly gives the voice of the soul. Long before the mind thought about purchasing or not purchasing the item, your soul knew whether it was "yes" or "no". And the moment the mind decides whether it is "yes" or "no" you will feel whether that Decision is aligned with the soul or not. But in reality, the very first time you look at something the soul already says "yes" or "no". *Then* the mind kicks in and starts analyzing. In cases in which your mind and your soul are saying *yes*, you can be 100% certain that you are looking at *your* piece of clothing and this piece of clothing will lead to good experiences. What if the soul says yes and the mind says no? In this case you can still purchase it but will have to process some doubts along the way. The only option that is absolutely detrimental is if your soul says *no*, and you buy it anyway. Your mind might be saying that it's convenient and functional or on sale or cheaper than something else...but if you don't actually like it, it will not bring you luck.

The ideal path is for your mind and your soul to both say yes. This is the path of least resistance and will yield the greatest results and the most ideal life-line. If you are in doubt, then it is not *yours*. No matter how things seem, no matter what people say in their "good advice"...they have no idea what is good for your soul. If you find yourself trying to convince yourself...then it's not yours either and you can re-decide to give the piece of clothing back.

The clothing that is truly *yours* you will not necessarily find in the most expensive of shops since the "posh culture" and it's illusion of prestige and "brand names" are mostly connected to the world-mind about which the soul doesn't really care. But even *if* your piece of clothing is to be found in a fancy and expensive shop, remember that "lack of money" is yet another illusion of the world-mind and that you have the opportunity to train your focus to not look at money but at what you *really* like. By looking at what you *really* like (rather than money), the money follows automatically. This might mean that you buy the piece and from somewhere an "unexpected" flow of money comes in to cover that. Not because you were focusing on money but because you were following flow.

This analogy applies to everything in life. You enter the shop (life) to have a look around, without setting up "grand tasks to achieve" or having to find something (neediness). You let go of your expectation to reach a certain goal. You do have a *general* image of what you want, but you don't crave it as you know it is waiting on you somewhere anyway and you can discern it from other peoples clothes (external/foreign goals). You're at ease. The moment your mind has made a decision, check what if *feels* like. How you feel at the moment of Decision never errs and is a 100% reliable tool to succeed in the world. Once you realize that, your entire life will become simplified and this book will have been worth the read. Rigid planning is not needed as you trust the stream of life and gently choose, claim and take that which you like.

Should you want to make a practical exercise out of this...then try it by the means of going shopping for clothes. Some readers may object: "Well, this might be easy when buying clothes, but it's a lot more difficult when it comes to jobs, relationships, health and spirituality. But seeing it as "difficult" is part of the very illusion. Anything that is "difficult" or too complicated is an indicator of you not being your true natural self. If something is native to you, then it does not involve suffering and hardship. Each of the "movie-scenes" you experience in everyday life are a metaphor for your relationship to your soul, and the fulfilment of your true desires is *much* easier than you think.

Remember that if you resisting a little thing, you are resisting everything, and if you appreciate a little thing, you are appreciating everything. Why? How so? Infinity does not discern between "little" and "big". If you are resisting hanging up washed clothes, in that moment you are emanating that energy out into the world, and that's who you are and what everything is. If you are enjoying and loving hanging up washed clothes, in that moment you are emanating that energy out into the world and will receive love back throughout the day.

Soft Intending

The more power you have the less effort you need to allow things to happen. In my own life I have implemented what I call "the soft touch" which involves doing less, planning less, working less...and being, experiencing, allowing *more.* The reason I haven't been eager to teach the technique in this section to my students is because it's much too simple for most people. It consists of writing down your intentions on a regular basis. That's it.

Now imagine someone visiting one of my Courses for a significant amount of money, hoping to find empowerment, relief, liberation and I say: "Well, simply write down your Intentions. That's all you need in order to experience beauty, success, wealth, well-being, health, love and happiness for the rest of your life." A bit too simple isn't it? I thought so too when I first heard of the idea more than 12 years ago. I dismissed it as naïve and went on to explore other things. Today I realize that I misunderstood the method.

Where your attention flows to on a regular basis, determines what you experience as reality. It therefore follows that by talking and writing about what you like and why you like these things on a daily basis, you will flow your attention in the appropriate directions.

By writing down your preferences on a daily basis you filter attention in a manner that the "universal field" will, from that list, deliver whatever is currently available and easy to manifest. This is "Reality Creating by Divine

Will" – you just leave it up to God what to deliver and not deliver and how or when to deliver it.

Too simple? Then we will now look at the "small print" of this and then *intend that intending works for you.*

"So, you recommend making goal lists?"

No. The technique of "Soft-Intending" or "Intention-Lists" is something radically different than goal lists. Goal-lists are made with the presupposition of something you only do once in awhile (such as on New Year), then you "achieve" and then you make a "new goal list". Intention-Lists are made every week or even every day. Goal-lists are based on conventional linear-thinking. Intention lists are not written with the idea that these intentions will happen "sometime in the future" but first I have to do this, and this and that in order to reach my goal". Goal-lists are also written in the presupposition that you have to "do" something for your goals. Intention-Lists are based on a different concept, namely that thought is cause of reality and not action. Intention-Lists serve to work at the cause (thought, attention) rather than the effect (action, physical objects and events). Action is a natural consequence of thought. Your job here is to align your thought with the desires of your soul. The rest happens (almost) by itself – automatically. You send out pulses of thought and the energy-field some call "Universe" answers by reflecting your thoughts as life. You radiate, life radiates back. The concept of a "goal", as indoctrinated by society, creates an artificial separation/polarization between today and the future (I sometimes use the word "goal" anyway because it's the word most are familiar with). In Consciousness (which is cause of reality) such separations do not exist. Sure, it may take awhile until your dreams come true, but you needn't add to this time-span by thinking of your goal as something "in the distant future". Intention-Lists you therefore do not make so that "something happens some day *out there*", but so that something happens *right now in you*. And because some change is happening within you can the external world respond to that. The external world is merely a reflection of your internal world. Actually everything happens within Consciousness anyway so there really is no "out there".

"So, all I have to do is write down my desires and they come true? When? How? From where?"

No. It doesn't work like this. When writing your intention lists you do this in a playful way, in the spirit of lightness, *without expectation* and without assigning too much importance to results. "Expectation" again implies a *split* between the now and the future. Your waiting for something to happen instead of enjoying *today.* So you write down what you'd like to experience, what you intend, but none of it *has to* happen. You could also do without. Neediness implies a separation from the object of desire. That's why we don't say "Wish-Lists" but *Intention*-Lists. Intend it but also be happy without it. Your only task is to define what you'd like to have, be, do. It is lifes task to deliver. And you'll be surprised at what it delivers. When practising this art you do not ask about the *how, when, where.* How, when and where block the stream of energy because they again create an artificial separation between here-now and some other time and place. Is this sinking in? Yes, when doing conventional goal-planning, of course you ask how you are going to achieve something, but these rules do not apply here. As soon as "how", "when", "from where" come into play, counter-intentions and doubts arise. But where you have no expectation of manifestation in the first place but are only playfully saying "It would be nice if X happened", there is no purpose for counter-intentions.

"So, should I phrase my intentions in the present?".

Relax. What is and is not appropriate is essentially determined by *you*. This is a playful and light-hearted technique and there is no space for strict rules. You can't do anything *wrong* in applying this. Even paying overly much attention to how you phrase something is indicative of not taking this lightly. Since this practice is done on a regular basis, you'll have plenty of opportunities to phrase and rephrase for something to "feel better". I personally phrase most of my intentions in the present or in the past-tense (as-if they've already happened) but sometimes, depending on my mood, I also use things like "I want" and "I'd like" and "I wouldn't mind if...". Wanting something implies a separation, but in some cases "wanting" may have the appropriate "soft touch" for that day. More often I use "I have", "I am" and "I do". When in an especially believing mood I use the past-tense and "remember" something having already come true. This frees the mind from goal-thinking, expectation and similar blocks. Another way of bypassing the mind-split is to use "I appreciate" or "I like" as ones intention-statements. "I appreciate" does not imply the separation that "I want" does. This is why I often add "Appreciation-Lists" to my Intention-Lists, writing down things that I already appreciate, that I am grateful for, that have already manifested in my life. This further serves to diffuse the separative difference between "reality" and "imagination". By not making much difference between what I'd like to become real and what is already real, I train my mind to accept that which was formerly "unrealistic".

"But don't I have to feel it in order for it to manifest?"

"Light Touch" involves not putting too much effort into this but just having fun. It is right that creating a pleasant feeling in your body equates pulsing energy into the field and that it is this energy that will yield results. You get this feeling by clearly defining your intention. However, you do not always have to "feel something". Some of my best results I received by pure intention without any conditions or prerequisites. If however, this is *much too simple* for you, you can strengthen your feeling (energy field) by asking *why* you want or intend something and answering that. The feeling often weakens when you ask how you will get something or when you will get something or from where you will get it. Listen closely to your body and you will notice how these questions often (not always!) weaken your intent (an exception is when it is obviously apparent *how* you will get something, then the how strengthens your intent). Intending is like ordering something in the Internet: Only the most neurotic minds would stop all their daily activity and *wait* for their product to be delivered or needing to know the details of how, from where and when it is delivered. We don't do that when Intending because we know we've ordered it, period. *We don't give it much thought after we've intended it.*

For some intentions I add *reasons why*. This I especially do with items on my list that have, in many variations, been part of my list for a long time (things that haven't manifested yet). "I'd like to have this, *because...*" and "I believe I can have this, *because...*" strengthens a thought, densifies it into a belief. The more reasons you find for something, the more you tend to believe it. Imagine a thought as the top of a table and the reasons as the legs of the table on which the thought stands, which it is *based* on. So indeed my intention lists are a mix of gratitude-lists, appreciation-lists, why-because lists and pure intentional-statements.

"Should I watch out what I intend for?"

With the soft-touch-technique, you do not have to watch out so much, because the field will only manifest what is in alignment with your soul and appropriate for the current time. It is recommended that you mix the small and big, the realistic and unrealistic, the outrageous and the mundane into the same list, in order to diffuse artificial separation. By "unrealistic" I do not mean intentions that do not fit to your souls path such as "I am the President of the country", but things that would truly fascinate or interest you. You do not intend for others because you cannot create reality for others. You can however intend for the benefit of others by wishing them well on your intention list or wishing yourself to experience that other person in a certain way.

"But isn't it better to focus on one or two things than on a huge list?"

For the Reality Creation Technique in the first chapter choosing only one or a few things to focus on is appropriate. These are methods that involve you as the main source of energy. The "Intention-List" method however, involves "higher forces and sources" as the creating factor. You write down many things and it chooses which of those things come to fruition This spreading of focus to many different things helps not to get too attached to your intention or to keep thinking about it (expectation). You are not putting all your eggs in one basket. If one thing does not manifest, another will.

The main purpose of this is however not the result itself, not the manifestation itself but your ability to focus your thoughts in preferred directions and being aware of your intentions on a daily basis. You can either live life on automatic and have the world determine where your attention goes, or you can decide. And during this exercise you decide where your thoughts go. Another side-effect is that you become aware of the fact that you can place intentions for just about anything. You can even place intentions on how you want your intentions to manifest.

Much energy is not actually wasted on the "big things" the "big goals" but on the little disturbances throughout a normal day...of which we forget that we can intend other things about them. The intention "To be rich" or "to have sexual adventures" is not appropriate while you are driving by car from point A to B. For this segment of your day there would be a more appropriate mini-intention such as: "I have a good and safe drive. The streets are free. I arrive feeling fresh and relaxed". These pre-thoughts pre-pave either this drive or future drives so that you needn't *compensate* by *doing* so much anymore. Most doing is only a compensation for bad thinking or failing to define your intention. If you're in a foul mood while driving because the streets are stuffed and you get a headache, you will have a lot of doing to do: Get some aspirin at the pharmacy. Get some more coffee to wake up. Change your clothes because you arrive sweaty. This would not happened would you have taken a few seconds to simply *define* what you prefer. So this is not even about the "big intentions" yet but about even having the idea that you can intend for certain things. Today I still receive emails from people (who are supposed to have learned the art of intending) in which I can see dozens of opportunities to *intend* in one single paragraph and hundreds intentions offering themselves in one single email. But the writers of these emails don't seem to notice. They seem to be of the opinion that

"that's just the way things are" without loosing a thought on the fact that they could be able to place new and different intentions. What is the use of stating problems without also stating what you intend to experience instead? There is no use in it. From a soul-perspective it does not make sense. Someone will write to me and say "My problem is...". And, if I've already taught this person Intending, I will respond with "Yes? And so?". And if they don't get it, they will respond with: "So, what should I do?" Then I will say: "How the heck should I know what you should do? Regarding the problem you write to me about, what do you *intend?*" As you might guess, people still need *a lot* of practice in shifting their attention.

"How does this mix with to-do-lists, weekly-plans, diaries?"

People have been conditioned to look at what *was* and what *is*...which is why they keep attracting more of what was and what is into their life. The purpose of regular intention-lists is to move that predisposition just a little. Because attention has been condition to observe what was and what is, change comes in snail pace. The brainwashing is intense and encompasses schools, religion, mass-media, culture, literature...and even "spirituality", and can only be shifted by regular practice. It is better to do to-do-lists, plans and diaries than nothing, because they involve conscious writing and contemplation. However, to-do-lists focus your attention on obligations, expectations the world has of you and not on your souls intentions. They mostly refer to things and errands you are "supposed to" take care of. But attention: There is nothing wrong with including some errands for the day on your intention list. Never should the to-do's be the basis or main part of your intention list though. There's two smart ways to add obligatory errands and to-do's to your intention list:

a) By stating the desired *outcome* of that To-Do (so instead of writing "I have to go repair the car" you write "The car is repaired for a good price and all is well" for example). This may lead to the To-Do being taken care of by someone else, "unexpectedly".

b) By specifically addressing the To-Do to the "universe", as something the "universe" should *take care of for you*. Yes, you do not have to do everything yourself, some things are taken care of "miraculously", as you will discover.

People who merely make "To-Do-Lists" end up in a state of Frustration because the damn list just never ends. And how could it? What you give attention to, accumulates. So if you do include actions onto your list then only such actions you feel like doing or by phrasing them in a way that includes the *outcome*.

Diaries are focussed on the past and create more of what you've already experienced. When you remember something you warm it back up again and open yourself for it or something similar happening again. So when you write a diary, it does help you remain aware of the contents of your mind and what is important to you. If you do insist to continue writing a diary, despite this chapter, then emphasize the good memories...and if you want, build in a few "imagined/invented memories".

That would be good reality-creation-practice. But if you are someone who enjoys writing a lot, then it would be even better if you write imaginary film-scripts or scenes or stories of what you would like to experience...as if real.

Weekly Plans or Monthly Plans are alright, but again: These are also often action- and realism-oriented. But if you insist on week-planning or if you need to do it in context of your company, then at least begin with the goal (the final outcome) and why you want it (the motivator) and then *work out your actions from that vantage point.* This is much more effective than starting out with an action list.

"Do I have to write them down? Can't I just repeat them as Affirmations?"

Repeating affirmations (such as "I am rich, I am rich, I am rich, I am rich, I am rich") and other "positive thinking" techniques have nothing to do with the technique of Intention-Lists. Every day something else will feel authentic and right and every day your Intentions change a little bit. Because of new experiences you make, your intentions become more specific, more general or simply different than before. It is important to choose statements and phrasings that are positive but also feel *authentic.*

If you choose Intentions beyond the calling of your soul ("I am the President of the U.S.") you are wasting your energy. Certain intentions will repeat themselves from day to day but the way you phrase it or a certain detail of that intention may change. Yesterday I wrote into my intention list that I want to increase my book sales, today I am writing that my books sales double. Yesterday you may have placed the intention of meeting a certain person and you did meet the person, but now you realize that your intention is not actually "meeting the person" but having a good time with him/her, so you rephrase it. The mix of positive-but-realistic (currently realistic) is the most effective type of intention. You are looking at what will probably manifest anyway, things you already believe to some extent anyway, and intend *them.* On a scale from 1 (very negative thought) to 10 (very positive thought) these would probably be "level 6" thoughts. Nevertheless do sometimes add a few level 5,7,8,9,10 items to your list.

It is never about controlling-the-mind or controlling-the-thoughts as some teach, it is about *gently guiding* them by writing down what feels good, what improves your general state. Why? What you feel determines what other thoughts you attract and accumulate. It is easier to improve an emotion that attracts 100 000 corresponding thoughts than trying to think each of these 100 000 thoughts deliberately. Wisdom will therefore not aim at "positive thinking", which is almost an impossible task, but at *positive feeling*. There are no rigid rules (not even the ones mentioned here) about how and what to write as long as it improves your vibratory frequency (emotion).

"OK, but if this really isn't just positive thinking, how do I handle the negative thinking that comes up all the time?"

You rephrase your negative thinking to what you want *instead*. That's how you incorporate it. Negative things coming up can immediately be integrated into your intention-lists. Every problem is also a desire. The most common mistake I see people make is naming problems without the intended alternative. In this sense they are actually intending the negative. How crazy is that? Problems and negativity are a natural part of earth-life and do have the purpose to allow us to more clearly define and shape how we flow energy. Every problem is an excellent opportunity to place our intentions more clearly. In a natural flow of things it works like this: A problem arises. From that, an intention arises. And from that an experience arises. If you are not yet content with that experience, you define a new intention or re-define the intention. Period. The mistake some make is: They experience something unpleasant, place an intention, and if they then again experience something unpleasant, they do not re-define their intention and think the problem "has won". Then they waste days or months pondering on the problem. But as far as I am concerned there is only

1. Experience

2. From that experience new intentions/desires arise.

3. Experience.

4. More intentions.

5. Experience.

6. Intend.

And so forth, forever and ever. The game never ends. And in this way you can define more and more precisely who you are. In time old facts are always replaced with new facts. But if the negative persists anyway, then you are dealing with something that is not truly negative but only labelled by you as such. It wants to be examined. It invites you to make friends with it. In such cases you can write about the problem...and write and write and write...and question...until it becomes clear what is going on behind-the-scenes of it, until it becomes clear why you are holding on to it. With the full creative control you have over your experience, you needn't shy away from the negative. You can embrace it, see what it means for you, examine it in a sincerely curious way and then let go by defining what you want instead.

"Do I really have to do this everyday?"

No. There are no rules, remember? Doing it every day is a recommendation for beginners and for those who are in a very low state. Pros may let weeks pass before they do their next intention list. I personally do it about once a week, no matter if things are going well or not. When you are in the flow and everything is going well, this entails that it is easier to continue being in the flow (like attracts like) and less intention will be necessary. However, even though you will intend less in good times, intentions very easily manifest in good times. Some will not intend because they don't want to "disturb the flow" of things. Some will not want to intend too often because they shy away from the awareness and the changes that go with it. It is OK and only human to put some brakes on the changes.

I personally have pledged to do this for the rest of my life, because awareness does make all the difference.

There is a flood of thoughts coming in on a daily basis...from the Internet, from other people, from TV, from neighbors...and most of the thoughts offered to you have nothing whatsoever to do with your souls path. So by practicing regular deliberate intention I keep in touch with spirit and filter in its intuitions. If you do not want the good life, then don't do this. But in understanding that your inner world is the cause of your external world, you'd normally be *eager* to use this tool. Knowing the workings of the world, you can't wait to do your next list! To label it as "difficult" misses the point that it actually makes everything easier if your thoughts are clear and orderly. Everything you have ever experienced first began as a thought.

"Resting on your Laurels" is a beginners mistake. Just because you have manifested something or achieved something big, does not mean that the rest will just be created all by itself. I recommend you keep on deliberately intending, even after some of your dreams have come true. It is fun to progress more and more and more and more.

Working on the fundamental underlying basis of things (thought) will make everything else easier. You will no longer require others to change their opinion or way of being. You will no longer require the world to change. Others will no longer have to conform to your way of seeing things. The world was intended as diversity and everyone chooses, by means of attention, which part of this diversity he/she filters in. Others have nothing to do with what you experience. You will be attracting more and more of that which you like. I will now end this chapter because it is more useful writing down your own intentions instead of reading mine.

Manifestation Experiences

I have already described many of my personal experiences in magic in many other books. This serves to give readers even more examples of what is actually possible in this life, because we so easily forget. All of these events happened to me personally just the way I describe them. Experiencing magic or something previously considered impossible ups your self-confidence and lowers your need of "proof" or the need of legitimization from others or "authorities". I will focus on events that happened from 2005-2010. (My financial, relationship, health and spiritual goals were already achieved previously to 2005, so I wont be going into the normal stuff much, although I do recommend you aim for the earth-basics of money, love and health first, before anything else).

The Atlantean Artefact

Names and Locations of this Account have been changed to protect individuals involved.

I sometimes add "impossible" items to my intention-lists. One of them, a few weeks ago was this: "Dear Universe, thank you for showing me an artefact from Atlantis that the world hasn't seen yet". I had zero expectation of this happening but it seemed like a funny thing to write down. Chances are that the sunken continent of Atlantis didn't even *exist*. But the ways of the Universe prove to be mysterious. Two weeks later I had already forgotten about the intention when I received an email from someone who had *no idea* of my intention, nor would he even know if I cared about Atlantis. He sent me the picture of a kind of vase that had been found by divers off the Coast of Long Island. The divers had found this artefact more than a 100 years ago...back in the days when divers still wore weighty helmets. The artefact had ended up in a Museum in New York City, without any note or indication what it was or where it was from. When that museum went broke on of the employees received the artefact to take it home with her. This woman passed it on to her son. It was her son that contacted me showing me the pictures of the artefact. He explained to me that he had taken it to the biggest auction houses in the United States and to the local university, but nobody had been able to estimate it's value or to even determine where it is from and which language was inscribed on it. If auctioneers cannot estimate it's value then that's because it is out-of-range of their reality, meaning either two low in value or much too high. Looking at the picture, my guess was that it was too high. It had various layers of "age" on it...mint-green, bronze, Gold. It looked incredibly old yet strangely intact. The local university confirmed the writing not to belong to any known language. They therefore lost interest in the artefact. "If it is not known, it must be a hoax". Finally it struck me that this was connected to the intention I had placed 2 weeks ago. A rush of excitement. What are the chances of this manifesting? 1 in a Billion? But make no mistake, it matters not whether this artefact is an actual Atlantis-artefact or not. What matters is that *something corresponding to my intent manifested*. The universe always delivers on the path of least resistance meaning it chooses *from what is available* and what most *resembles* the intention. So, supposing that Atlantis didn't even exist...the universe is able to deliver something on the intention *anyway*! Someday, if I feel the inspiration, I might take the trip to visit the guy and find out more about the vase. Until then I rest excitedly in the knowledge that even the most outrageous intention is responded to.

Pre-Cognitive Dream

A few weeks ago I dreamed of two women that I had never seen. One was a red-haired woman, who appeared first in the dream, the other was a black-haired woman, who appeared second and seemed to be observing me and the red-haired woman. Both were somehow admiring something about me in that dream, but I couldn't tell what. Upon awakening they were still vividly in my awareness and I went to take a shower wondering who they were and what the dream could possibly mean. That day I was scheduled to do a Coaching for a group in a downtown building. At around 10 o'clock the red-haired woman entered the rooms. She was not there for my coaching but visiting the owner of that company. I stood in the "coffee room" stunned. She must have noticed the awkward look on my face because she smiled at me. This was not a woman that was "a bit similar" to the one I dreamed of the night before, but the *exactly same one*. I didn't tell her I had dreamed of her lest she misunderstand it as some creepy hit-on. She was Spanish and hardly spoke any English, but we exchanged

Smalltalk the best we could. And then she was off into another room. I stood there considering what had happened. Pre-cognitive dreaming had happened to me many times before, but just like many times before, I had forgotten all about it and it took me by surprise all over again. The linear mind is a curious thing. It will sometimes easily forget, trivialize or ignore the most lucid states of awareness. Standing there I understood that the second black-haired woman would probably be showing up too. And some hours later she did. I went back to the coffee room in the afternoon and she was sitting there talking to someone else. She too smiled when she saw me, almost as if in recognition. Had I been in her night dream like she had been in mine? Quite possible. We seem to meet different kind of people on dreamscape, some of which we don't even know in our waking life. We too exchanged a brief chat about this and that and when I returned to my room I was beaming with fascination by the occurrence. I tried to explain what had happened to my group, but they did not find it as entertaining as I did. Maybe it reminded them that they had not experienced a pre-cognitive dream recently. Maybe they thought I was making it up. Or people just don't care about other peoples dreams and understandably so. In any case, maybe I ought to stop being surprised about it and just take it for granted by examining my dreams more closely. In this way it may occur more often. What did the dream mean? It doesn't matter what it meant. No need to do a "dream interpretation". As far as things developed it didn't mean anything because I never saw the women again after that…neither in my dreams nor in waking-state. What does matter though is the fact that time is so much more fluid and non-linear than we believe. And *that* is exciting.

Synchronicities Stacking Up

This story is not spectacular but it is rather funny because it shows what intense focus of attention can lead to. In October 2006 I was conducting a "Business English Course" for a company that does civil engineering and construction and building planning. During the three weeks I was conducting courses I was immensely focussed on Vocabulary and Concepts that concern Construction, Building and Engineering. I became aware of procedures and words I had never heard of before (having to learn the words I was supposed to teach my students). In the November and December weeks after these lengthy courses I had several registrations for single-sessions of Reality Creation Coachings. This was nothing new. What was new were the professions that these people had. Without having any relation to the construction planning company I had worked for, they *all* related to buildings, building, real estate or architecture! No, not some of them, but for the remainder of 2006 *all* of them. There was a House builder from Germany, another building planner from Austria, an architect from Seattle, a real estate agent from Sydney, another home builder from England and another architect from Toronto, Canada. There were really a few more related to buildings and building but I don't remember their exact professions. Some might think that this is due to satisfied customers referring others, but I have established that none of these clients had anything to do with each other. I asked them if they knew person x and company x but they didn't. They found out about me either from my books, my website or from lectures I gave. This was an excellent example of "coincidences" referring to the same or a similar topic (building) stacking up on each other. The more you focus on something, the more of something you get. The more of something you get, the even more of something you get. Energy is accumulative. This was by no means the only occurrence of that kind but served as an "in your face" example of Synchronicity.

The Woman from the Billboard Ad

I was travelling to Zurich, Switzerland on some business I had to conduct. I took the train instead of the car so that I would have enough free attention to conduct some Meditations. In the train I applied a marathon *reality creation technique* session to up my vibe. By the time the train arrived at its final destination I was feeling high as an eagle. The mind was quite blissfully empty while I rushes of energy went through the spine and elating tingling sensations in my head and solar plexus. My perception was such, that everything seemed brighter and sparkling. I stood at the train station for awhile, observing with fascination. I was quite obviously in an altered state of consciousness. I could stare at the most mundane object with fascination, no trace of boredom or impatience. Enlarged pupils, the eyes of a little child, wandering around looking, listening. Sounds appeared warmly filtered, meaning even noise didn't sting or make me react in a nervous way. I walked passed a billboard ad featuring the most gorgeous looking woman I had *ever* seen. It was an ad for jewellery and the brunette, brown-eyed lady looked out mysteriously at the pedestrians. I stood there and thought: "Well, I wouldn't mind meeting her today". Little did I know that I *would* be meeting her that day. After I had conducted my business I returned to the train station in the evening and took a seat in my train. I was no longer on my meditation-high as I was that morning, but still felt quite refreshed and mentally acute. As you might have guessed, the brunette model entered the part of the train I was in. I did not recognize her as the model from the billboard though. I had completely forgotten that ad and the events of that morning. Although there must have been more than 30 free seats to sit at (there was nobody else in the part of the train) she approached me and asked if she could sit right across from me. Quite obviously she wanted to strike up a conversation during a long ride back to Milan (I was staying in Italy at the time). We did converse and eagerly so. The train started filling up and we were so immersed in our conversation that we didn't even notice that the train had become full. Somehow we had managed to talk for a whole hour without even telling each other what our professions were. Now *that's* a good conversation…when you forget to define oneself over a profession or place of origin. Finally our jobs were brought up and she told me she worked as a Model. She said something to the extent of: "Maybe you have seen the billboard ad all over Zurich. The one with the jewellery." In that very moment it struck me like lightning. It was her. It *was* her! The pulses of energy I had felt that morning returned, oscillating and flowing and vibrating through my body. I had created this. "Yes, I saw the ad this morning and thought 'I wouldn't mind meeting her' I admitted". She found this quite interesting and started talking about how thoughts sometimes become real − a conversation I could truly relate to. The train had arrived at its final destination, everyone had already left, but our eyes and emotions were still interlocked as we remained on our seats not noticing our surroundings. I broke the spell by saying "The train is already empty". We walked along the platform curiously silent, realizing that we had just experienced a magical encounter out of the blue and would probably never see each other again. At the end of the platform we were about to hug each other or exchange phone numbers but we resisted the urge to break the spell and said our goodbyes, both turning around several times while walking away. "What was that all about?" the clueless mind asked. It was being in love for just a few hours and with a complete stranger.

Music from Beyond

In 2007 I built up a little home music studio to produce music for meditation mainly. There were phases and weeks I was so immersed in that creative work that I would get up in the morning at 9 and sit at the keyboard, computer and other equipment until 3 in the morning, day after day. On some days I overdid it, neglecting my other work, my partner and friends. My attention was clearly lost in music. Loosing yourself in something, immersing attention has the benefit of really getting things done and the disadvantage of not doing everything else that has to be done. It was during this time I started having dreams about music at night. But one of these many dreams was different. In it I was completely lucid and aware of dreaming. I was floating through a universe made of sound. It was some kind of astral plane in which the most awesome types of sounds were accompanied by energy swirls, sweeps, sparkles, clouds, dust, geometric formations of the most intense colours and shapes. As I drifted through this universe of sound I felt elated beyond imagination. The elation of being on a higher spiritual plane was not new to me, but the musical aspect was. There were some unseen beings accompanying me. I felt there presence and acknowledged them as something like mentors. "Why don't you transfer some of this sound to your world?" one of them suggested. "Listen carefully" another explained. As the dream continued it did become quite clear that they wanted me to try to "channel" certain music of this plane "back down" to earth. And I fully agreed, because I liked what I heard. "I don't know if I have the means and skill to replicate this kind of music" I recall myself saying (most astonishing to me personally was that I was still able to produce doubts in my elated state of awareness). I was lucid enough to recall the entire conversation…something rather rare, as one mostly forgets a dream once waking up. "Let it come" a third being suggested. "Make it similar" the first one chimed in. "Yes, I get the overall feel of this" I offered. There was much more said and explained but I leave that to your imagination. I awoke feeling like a helium balloon, a wide grin on my face. I laughed frequently throughout the day. The sounds fresh in memory I started looking for them in the millions of soundfonts my music and synth software had. It took an entire day to compose a single element of music. Maybe a musician "downloads" certain concepts and combinations from the field of consciousness. What is downloaded is filtered by one's on specific taste and preferences, but at the end of the day, all music is Divine.

Teaching my Teacher

This occurrence taught me how silly our concepts of rank and order can be. This does not mean that I believe that everyone is "the same" - I do appreciate and respect everyone to be unique. But sometimes that respect turns into a false sense of someone being "way up there". It was early morning when I received a phone call from across the Atlantic. Someone had read my book "Parallel Universes of Self" and wanted to have me as a personal coach for a few days. I had just woken up and felt a bit groggy and therefore didn't put too much interest into the conversation…at first. "What was your name again?" I asked. That's when I realized that this "someone" was one of the most famous and highly regarded spiritual teachers and motivational speakers on the planet. I woke up pretty suddenly. "Is this a joke?" I was thinking at first. I will omit the name of the Teacher here to protect his identity. The funny thing was, that I was a *fan* of this Teacher and had used some of *his* teachings in my own books that he was referring too as "a brilliant"! I had not mentioned his name in my books, nevertheless his influence was in there. So there I was, standing in my living room in my underwear and a dirty t-shirt, unshaven, uncombed being asked my one of my idols to coach him. "Alright, how about a 2-day get-together?" I heard myself say, getting my act together. "That'll be fine. I wouldn't mind grabbing a beer with you and just talking, but I'd also like to help me with an issue that a normal counsellor wouldn't grasp."

And so it happened. And why not? He gives so much to people he needs to make sure he is on the receiving end too sometimes. He arranged and paid for the flight. We had not agreed on a coaching rate but after our session ended he paid more generously than he would have had to. I spent some of the flight-time meditating on the coaching-session, ridding myself of my beliefs of inferiority. The trick was not to think of him as my teacher, but as a mere human being that needs some assistance too. And that did the trick. We met as equals.

To some coffee and breakfast we exchanged experiences in the new-age-business, a few hearty laughs and then rapidly proceeded to the issue he was dealing with. And the issue was indeed "out of this world" and on that morning I really couldn't imagine anyone other than me coaching him on that. The guy was about 100 000 times as famous as me, 10 Million times as rich, but this specific issue could not be addressed with money.

One thing I am good at is spontaneous-coaching, which develops approaches not based on a script but according to what is happening right now. This is almost a little like "channelling". We met on day two realizing that the issue had already been solved entirely the day before.

What made this experience special for me was not the "who" of the outside persona as displayed in the media, but the fact that the issue was incredibly advanced (dealing with parallel universes) and how exhilarating it was to be *the only person alive* who could help with it. You too, dear reader, have certain abilities and knowledge that are unique to you, that nobody else can give to the world. And it can be exhilarating to discover what those skills are.

A Weighty Issue

Attention had always been a little stuck on the issue of weight and overweight throughout my life. I had never quite been my ideal weight. In some phases of my life I didn't care. In other phases I was concerned. In others I tried to change my eating habits. In others I tried Reality-Creation-Technique. In others a tried a lot of physical movement. I tried the occasional diet. On other occasions I ridiculed people who always talk about diets but never loose weight. And on occasion I ridiculed those who even care about weight. But ideal weight never ever really stabilized. The "I don't care about weight" was a lie because if I really didn't care about weight why would I even have to mention that I don't care? There always had been some attention stuck there for the main reason that "If I'm so good at reality creation, why is weight still an issue? Why hasn't reality creation been working on that?" So one day I finally decided to quit, just like I had decided to quit smoking half a year previously. I used the reality-creation-technique described in the first chapter, again, but this time not half-heartedly like I had done before, but with the firm intention to use-it-until-it-works.

An so it went. "I allow myself to loose two more pounds in the next four days". I went in small steps. And if the two pounds did not happen, I kept going on. New information started popping up. Someone recommended a diet to me I had never heard of, one so rare that books on it weren't even available in English. I took that information as a direct response of the Universe to my Intention. And that particular diet sped up the weight loss (no need to write to me asking what it was – if you do Intentions properly, the diet that is best for *you* will come to you). After quitting smoking I had unnoticeably gained a massive 30 pounds, which were lost within 3 months. The ideal weight has meanwhile stabilized. It still requires some effort to maintain (physical movement and maintaining my new eating habits), but that effort will be no more in another few months when I am fully accustomed to that weight.

I mention this story to tell readers that it sometimes really does require for you to go the extra mile, invest the extra focus to get the job done. Persistence is a wonderful thing.

A beautiful add on to this story is that I was actually able to "prove" the creation of this reality to students at a Course when I told them "I will send a Video to you in 3 months, showing you that I have lost 30 pounds". This, on the other hand, inspired them to breakthrough old limitations of their own.

Surfing to the Holy Grail
Locations undisclosed to protect the uninvolved

This is an example of how life can be when you just go with the flow, break routines or let go of trying to be so smart and allow the Universe to guide you. When you live without resistance you are always taken to nice places. When you live without expectation, you are always surprised.

In the summer of 2009 I had been spending several weeks Windsurfing on a lake of stunning beauty, with a view of the Mountains, in Central Europe. As a Windsurfing Beginner (it was my first year) I had set the goal to reach a certain Island that appeared just a little further away than I might be able to handle. One morning I decided to go for it. I packed a water-tight backpack with a t-shirt, jeans and some water and food and went Windsurfing with my backpack, all the way to that Island, not even knowing if Wind-Circumstances would ever take me and the Surfboard back to the Surf-Station (who I borrowed the Board from). Having arrived at the Island I sat down for half an hour just resting, trying to make out the starting point back on mainland with the naked eye. I could barely do so, so I had indeed travelled far by Board.

From the distance the island looks like just some regular island you have on large lakes. This lake had several islands. I got the shoes and clothes from the backpack so that I could take a walk. Venturing into my island, to my great amazement there were not only ancient Celtic ruins in one part of it, but there was also a huge 18th Century castle on it, along with a royal park and incredible fountains, statues, hedges, buildings and brilliant works of art. I left the surf-board back at the water and took a tour of the Castle as the sole tourist that was there at that time. As if this day didn't already look like something out of a movie, I had a guide and the castle to myself. Turns out that it is one of the castles where the "Holy Grail" is rumoured to be.

In a daze of amazement I returned to my Board. Who would have guessed that what starts out as a simple round of Surfing, turns into the quest for the Holy Grail? Right there and then I intended to next time try to surf to an even further away island to see what awaits me there!

In any case, the wind was not allowing me to quite reach the spot I had started off at. In fact, if there wouldn't be a change (and weather does not change that quickly around this lake) I'd have to be hand-carrying Board and Sail for a mile or more. That was a prospect I was not looking forward to after having spent such a surprising day. I applied a few rounds of "Releasing Resistance" while keeping an eye on the place I intended to reach and, of course, did end up right where I set off.

Passive Income

Passive Income is a wonderful thing. It means you have things that are making money for you, covering your regular expenses. It means you do not have to work for money and the only work you do is work coming from joy, creativity, service-to-the-world rather than lack. I passed the mark from "working for money" to "being able to live off passive income" at the age of 30, having originally set the goal at the age of 28. Although this is no "spectacular manifestation" and I used no RCT for it (I merely used common sense) it is nevertheless the Basis of me having time to devote my life to spirituality, life coaching, book writing and so on. If you can find an asset or a product or an idea that makes money for you once you've produced it, and if that income covers all of your regular expenses, you can be considered rich. I do not consider you rich if you have to slave and be unhappy in order to earn a lot of money. Prosperity is not really about money its about being able to do what you want to do *when* you want to do it and having all the resources available *when* you need them.

A Final Word

Enjoy your trip through life. Nothing written in this book is a substitute for your own common sense and power. If you ever find something that works even better than RCT or Intending, use it! Life has its ups and downs but if you know of how energy works it can also be fantastic fun. Be well and may all your dreams come true!

Recommendations for Further Study

Frederick Dodson / Parallel Universes of Self (2007)

Frederick Dodson / Levels of Energy (2010)

www.realitycreation.org

ABOUT THE AUTHOR

Frederick E. Dodson, born in the USA 1974 currently lives in Arizona. He loves viewing life from many different viewpoints and putting spiritual knowledge into the practice of everyday life rather than following the 9-to-5 routine of a "steady job". In his twenties he wrote and published 15 books and held many hundreds of workshops, talks and seminars on the topic of reality creation. Lately however, he has retreated from teaching somewhat and only conducts one course a year. He has started viewing "experiencing joy" higher than "teaching others". Why? Because everyone has their own version of the truth and the purpose of his life is not to get others to agree with him, but to have fun. His favourite activities in the meantime include scuba diving, surfing the internet, writing, collecting movies, travelling and lucid dreaming.

If you liked this book and want to learn more, check out my website at www.realitycreation.org.

Made in the USA
Middletown, DE
15 July 2022